AIR CAMPAIGN

FRANCE 1940

The first great clash of World War II airpower

JAMES S. CORUM | ILLUSTRATED BY GRAHAM TURNER

OSPREY PUBLISHING
Bloomsbury Publishing Plc
Kemp House, Chawley Park, Cumnor Hill, Oxford OX2 9PH, UK
29 Earlsfort Terrace, Dublin 2, Ireland
1385 Broadway, 5th Floor, New York, NY 10018, USA
E-mail: info@ospreypublishing.com
www.ospreypublishing.com

OSPREY is a trademark of Osprey Publishing Ltd

First published in Great Britain in 2025

A catalogue record for this book is available from the British Library.

ISBN: PB 9781472864833; eBook 9781472864840;
ePDF 9781472864819; XML 9781472864826

25 26 27 28 29 10 9 8 7 6 5 4 3 2 1

Maps by www.bounford.com
Diagrams by Adam Tooby
3D BEVs by Paul Kime
Index by Richard Munro
Typeset by PDQ Digital Media Solutions, Bungay, UK
Printed by Repro India Ltd.

Title page: see caption on p.16.

Osprey Publishing supports the Woodland Trust, the UK's leading woodland
conservation charity.

To find out more about our authors and books visit www.ospreypublishing.com. Here
you will find extracts, author interviews, details of forthcoming events and the option to
sign up for our newsletter.

CONTENTS

INTRODUCTION   4

CHRONOLOGY   7

ATTACKER'S CAPABILITIES   11

DEFENDER'S CAPABILITIES   23

CAMPAIGN OBJECTIVES   41

THE CAMPAIGN   44

ANALYSIS AND CONCLUSION   89

BIBLIOGRAPHY   92

INDEX   95

INTRODUCTION

Spring 1940 saw a clash between three great powers: Germany, Britain, and France. In a campaign that surprised the world, it took less than six weeks for Germany to decisively defeat powerful British and French armies and air forces, ultimately forcing France to surrender. The German victory in spring 1940 can be attributed to Germany's generally very effective use of airpower, versus France and Britain's generally ineffective use of airpower. The defeat of France and Britain in 1940 was effected by the German Panzer breakthrough at Sedan on 13 May, and yet the German breakthrough that sealed the fate of France and the British Expeditionary Force (BEF) was only possible through the German use of airpower, which at Sedan was the largest single air battle of history to that point.

This book focuses on the operational level of air war as it evolved from World War I. In 1914, airpower played a minor, ancillary role in the armed forces of the European powers. But by 1918, the air forces of the major powers, which were still under command of the ground armies, now played an essential role in the combined-arms forces that had evolved during the war. Yet even in 1918, while airpower was an essential arm of the armies, it was still not considered to be a full partner with the ground forces.

British and French air doctrine had made little progress in terms of army/air and navy/air operations by 1940. The British and French air forces had gone down the doctrinal rabbit hole of strategic bombing theory, which postulated that bombing the enemy homeland was the only way in which airpower could achieve quick and decisive results in modern warfare. The Germans, however, had also evaluated the World War I experience but come to completely different conclusions. Even before Germany could field an air force, the German Army and its Shadow Air Staff had determined that effective military power required a large, multi-purpose air force that could operate as a close partner with the ground army and still conduct a strategic bombing campaign. When the Germans built the Luftwaffe, they had some specialist Stuka units and close-battle units that specialized in conducting air operations in close support of the ground armies. However, the fleet of twin-engine light and medium

bombers could perform both functions, one day with the Luftwaffe bombing enemy troop concentrations on the front lines, and the next day bombing rail centres, airfields, and ports deep inside France. It was the ability to do both things well that enabled the German victory in 1940.

This book looks closely at the senior military and air force leadership of the powers, as it was the leaders whose policies determined the size and composition of the air forces plus the doctrine that they would use to employ those air forces. In 1940, the British and French were closely matched in their ground forces. As to their divisions, Britain and France had the same number of armoured and motorized divisions in 1940 as the Germans did. Moreover, the Allied ground forces were superior in many respects. The French had considerably more, and better tanks than the German Panzer forces in 1940. The French also possessed a much larger number of heavy artillery pieces. In addition, half of the French border was protected by the extremely powerful fortresses of the Maginot Line.

It was in the air that the Germans had the advantage, with over 3,000 combat aircraft assembled into two air fleets and another thousand transport, light reconnaissance, and liaison aircraft. So, on the Allied northern front, the Germans had numerical superiority. But the numbers do not tell the whole story. During the 1940 battle, Britain maintained its Bomber Command, which amounted to 200–300 medium bombers that could be brought into the battle as readily as the German light and medium bomber forces, which were based in Germany. France and Britain both maintained hundreds of fighter aircraft deep in the rear to protect their cities against possible German attack. But these aircraft were also available to serve at the front. France had a severe shortage of modern aircraft in the 1940 campaign, but this was a completely self-inflicted wound. France had purchased hundreds of American fighter planes and light bombers starting in 1938. During the 1940 campaign, more than 200 American-built bombers were sitting in the rear because the dysfunctional French Air Force logistics and repair system had not got around to fitting them with bombsights, bomb release gear, radios, or armament. It was only in late May of

A Breguet 690 light bomber. The Breguet 693 was developed by the French Air Force as a light twin-engine attack bomber. It was fast, with a top speed of 300mph, and armed with two 20mm cannon and one 7.5mm machine gun, firing at the rear for defence. It could carry 1,000lb of bombs. The Breguets were intended to form assault groups for low-level attacks, but due to the poor reliability of their engines, deployment was long delayed, and l'Armée de l'Air received its first Br 693s in March 1940. Five Breguet squadrons of the French Air Force first flew operationally on 12 May 1940 against German columns in the Maastricht area. German flak shot down ten of 18 Br 693s on their first mission that very day. Later, the Breguets would bomb from higher altitudes to reduce flak losses, but as the Breguet bomber lacked a bombsight, its bombing tended to be inaccurate. (Alamy)

A French Potez 63 fighter/ light bomber. In the 1938 French rearmament plans, l'Armée de l'Air placed great hopes on the Potez 63, which had been designed as a heavy fighter, equivalent to Germany's Bf 110. The French Air Force also intended to use the Potez 63 with a three-man crew as its main reconnaissance plane. Some versions of the Potez 63 were also modified as light bombers, as it was heavily armed with seven forward-facing machine guns and could carry 450lb of bombs. Like most French aircraft, it was underpowered and had a disappointing max speed of 264mph. As a fighter, it was 80mph slower than a Bf 109 or a Bf 110, and it was not very effective either in the reconnaissance or ground attack roles. (IWM)

1940 – after the campaign had already been decided – that a handful of these American-made bombers, fully equal to the Luftwaffe's aircraft, were deployed to combat. Hundreds more French bombers and fighters also remained in rear depots because they had not been fully equipped for war. If not for the French Air Force logistics system, France would have had at least 300 more modern bombers and 200–300 more modern fighters at the opening of the campaign. France's notable failure to have an adequate combat air force was due solely to the French High Command, which over the years had failed to take serious notice of its air force's deficiencies and fix them.

France and Britain went into World War II thinking that it was an extension of 1918. Army/air coordination and C2 (Command and Control) were weak, and indeed, little different from 1918. Neither France nor Britain had developed any coherent operational doctrine for coordinating armies and air forces in the ground battle. In contrast, Germany had a practical doctrine of army and air cooperation as a central tenet of its way of war. The German doctrine was grounded in, and validated by, large-scale combat operations in the Spanish Civil War and in Poland in 1939, where German methods had brought decisive victory on the battlefield. The German command and control system made it possible to respond quickly and effectively to meet the operational conditions on a rapid-moving and fluid campaign.

Spring 1940 was a definitive moment in airpower history. During the next two years after the campaign, Britain and the United States would develop air forces and organizations, command and control systems and doctrine to effectively coordinate ground and airpower, all following the German models of command and control and doctrine employed in the 1940 campaign. By 1943, the British and American air forces would field airpower on a scale – and with an effectiveness – that went far beyond the Germans in 1940.

CHRONOLOGY

1933

30 January Adolf Hitler comes to power as Chancellor of Germany, establishes an Air Ministry, essentially a disguised Luftwaffe General Staff, and begins aerial rearmament by ordering thousands of trainers and fighters ('sport planes') and hundreds of bombers ('mail planes') based on prototypes already developed by the Shadow Air Staff within the German Army. In 1933, the German aviation industry would increase from 3,200 workers to more than 11,000 workers, with another 5,700 in the aircraft engine companies. Hitler's first armaments program results in 4,021 aircraft built in 1934–35. The expansion of the aviation industry will allow for mass production of more modern aircraft.

1935

Britain, alarmed by the rise of German military power, begins a major aerial rearmament effort that will result in production of the Hurricane and Spitfire fighters, the Wellington medium bomber, and the beginning of heavy bomber development.

1 March Hitler announces the official establishment of the Luftwaffe as a branch of the German armed forces, with over a thousand aircraft available.

1936

1 April The new Luftwaffe already possesses 1,000 bombers, several hundred fighters, and 1,000 training aircraft.

May In France, the Popular Front comes to power and Pierre Cot becomes Air Minister. A plan to build 1,500 new aircraft is approved by the government, and the goal is to increase the French bomber forces to 60 groups, with 720 aircraft, by 1939.

July The Spanish Civil War begins. Germany sends a 5,000-man, 100-aircraft aerial force called the Condor Legion to support the Spanish Nationalists. During the course of the war, which ends in March 1939, Germany will rotate 20,000 Luftwaffe personnel through the Spanish War to test new prototype aircraft such as the Messerschmitt Bf 109, the Junkers Ju 87 Stuka, the Heinkel He 111 bomber, the Dornier Do 17 bomber, and other aircraft models under combat conditions, fighting the most modern fighter and bomber aircraft of the Soviet Union, supporting the Spanish Republicans. By the end of the war, the Luftwaffe has extensive combat experience in close support, transport operations, and bomber operations.

1937

December Germany is now producing more than 300 military aircraft per month, and Britain between 175–200 aircraft per month, while a shortage of funding and the weak status of the newly nationalized French aircraft industry can only manage between 30–50 aircraft per month.

1938

Early 1938 General Joseph Vuillemin is appointed French Air Force Chief of Staff.

February A French Air Force mission arrives in the United States to purchase American aircraft. A hundred Curtiss H 75 fighters, then in production for the US Army Air Corps, are ordered. France's aviation industry is so far behind both the Germans and the British that purchases of American military aircraft become a key part of French aerial rearmament.

March The Plan 5 Air Rearmament Plan is approved by the French government. The French Air Force front-line strength is to expand to 2,617 modern aircraft by March 1941, with large reserves of fighters and bombers.

December The first Curtiss H-75s arrive in France. More are ordered and by August 1939, the French Air Force will have 176 H-75s on hand.

1939

February The French government orders 100 Martin 167s and 100 Douglas DB-7s as light bombers, with deliveries to begin June 1939.

1 September Germany invades Poland. World War II begins on 3 September when Britain and France declare war against Germany. In less than a month the German Army crushes the Polish Army, in its first modern Blitzkrieg campaign. The Luftwaffe, through extensive close air support, interdiction, and air superiority missions, plays a central role in the rapid success of German arms. However, at the end of the campaign, over 100,000 Polish soldiers will cross into neutral Romania and make their way to Britain and France to continue the fight against Germany. This includes thousands of Polish air force personnel and hundreds of pilots.

October The German Army and Luftwaffe forces that fought in the Polish campaign are redeployed to western Germany to face the British and the French. Hitler orders the OKH and Luftwaffe to begin planning for the invasion of the Low Countries and France.

29 October The first plan for the western offensive, called *Fall Gelb* (Case Yellow), is issued. The German plan is to advance into the Netherlands and Belgium, occupy those countries, and push British and French forces back into northern France.

November 1939–April 1940 German invasion plans for *Fall Gelb* are postponed more than a dozen times due to poor weather conditions.

10 January A Messerschmitt Bf 108 courier plane belonging to Luftflotte 2 accidentally strays into Belgian airspace and crash-lands. In the plane is a copy of the German *Fall Gelb* plan, which confirms the Allied High Command's view that the Low Countries are Germany's major objective.

February General Erich von Manstein, Army Group A's *(Heeresgruppe A)* Chief of Staff, proposes a new plan that would place most of Germany's Panzer motorized divisions in the centre of the German front to strike through the Ardennes, cross the Meuse at Sedan, and race across France to the Channel, thus cutting off the BEF and the French Northern Army Group, the best divisions in the Allied forces.

24 February Hitler approves a new version of *Fall Gelb*, to be executed by the army and Luftwaffe.

20 March General Gamelin, French Commander-in-Chief and Chief of the Allied Supreme War Council, approves a plan for the French First Army Group and BEF to advance into Belgium and assume a powerful

Air Vice Marshal C. H. B. Blount, Commander of the RAF component of the British Expeditionary Force (BEF), at his headquarters. (IWM)

defensive position on the Dyle–Breda line, as the Allied strategy in case Germany invades the Low Countries.

9 April Germany invades Denmark and Norway in a combined sea-land-air offensive, but Britain and France commit naval forces and ground troops to Norway. By early May, Denmark and most of Norway are firmly in German hands, Allied forces having retreated with heavy losses. British and French task forces remain only at Narvik. Again, the Germans prove their superior ability to coordinate air and ground forces and maintain a high tempo in the offence.

10 May The German invasion of the Low Countries begins. Germany initiates the attack with large airborne landings in the Netherlands, most of which quickly fail due to fierce and immediate Dutch counterattacks. Half of the Luftwaffe's 400-plane transport force is disabled. British-French forces advance immediately into Belgium and the southern Netherlands to establish the Dyle–Breda defensive line. Elsewhere, the Germans seize key bridges and river crossings, at Maastricht and the Albert Canal, and General von Kleist's VIII Division task force of Panzer and motorized divisions (*Panzergruppe Kleist*) advances through the Ardennes, facing only light resistance from the Belgians and French cavalry screening forces. The Luftwaffe undertakes an air superiority campaign by attacking dozens of Allied airfields, but the German attacks have relatively little effect on l'Armée de l'Air and the RAF stationed in France.

12 May The German advance in the Low Countries continues through the Ardennes. Von Kleist's Panzergruppe reaches the forests above Sedan and the Meuse in the afternoon of 12 May. The RAF and Belgian Air Force send bombers against the Albert Canal bridges that the Germans have surrounded with flak guns. Allied aircraft take severe losses and fail to inflict any damage.

13 May There is heavy fighting in the southern Netherlands and western Belgium as German Panzer forces collide with French tanks and mechanized forces.

13 May Von Kleist attacks across the Meuse to seize a bridgehead. The three Panzer divisions at Sedan are supported by more than 3,000 Luftwaffe aircraft sorties in a day-long attack that succeeds in suppressing the French defences, allowing the Germans to put bridges across the Meuse in the night of the 13th.

14 May Luftflotte 2 bombs Rotterdam, inflicting heavy damage and killing 900 civilians. The Netherlands surrenders.

The Germans advance four to six miles from their bridgehead. Guderian's XIX Panzerkorps pushes ahead against at times fierce but poorly coordinated French defence efforts.

Finally aware of the crisis, the French and British air forces carry out a series of attacks by French and British bombers, supported by fighter escorts. The attacking Allies take enormous losses. Over 50% of the British bombers are lost, and the German bridges remain operational. Heavy Allied losses are mostly attributed to the heavy concentration of Luftwaffe flak guns dedicated to supporting Von Kleist.

16 May After advancing beyond the Meuse bridgehead, OKH orders Panzergruppe von Kleist to halt its advance, fearing that Von Kleist's divisions will get too far ahead of the following infantry corps that would protect the German flanks.

17 May The newly established French Fourth Armoured Division under Colonel de Gaulle attacks Von Kleist's flank at Montcornet. After initial success, the Fourth Armoured is halted and then forced to withdraw under heavy bombardment by VIII Fliegerkorps Stukas.

18 May OKH revokes the halt order, allowing Von Kleist to begin his final advance to the English Channel. The German Fourth Panzerkorps advances on Lille, and the RAF and l'Armée de l'Air heavily engage in air battles around Lille with the Luftwaffe.

19 May Von Kleist's advance progresses rapidly. General Gamelin is relieved as Commander-in-Chief of the French Armed Forces and replaced with General Maxime Weygand. The AASF (The RAF Advanced Air Striking Force) is ordered to abandon France along with most of the RAF in France. Three fighter squadrons and a wing of Blenheim bombers remain in France, now moving south to Troyes.

20 May Panzergruppe von Kleist reaches the Channel at Abbeville so that the BEF and the French 1st and 7th Armies are now cut off from the rest of France.

22 May The XIX Panzerkorps begins its advance along the Channel coast. Boulogne and Calais, both with

British and French garrisons, are put under siege by two Panzer divisions. The RAF Fighter Command is now sending patrols from 11 Group based in southern England, and the Luftwaffe reports engaging large numbers of RAF fighters. German fighter and Stuka units are now operating from captured airfields in Belgium and northern France, notably Charleville, Guise, and Saint-Pol.

22 May The BEF mounts an attack with 57 tanks and four battalions with one French cavalry battalion in support. The attack has initial success, but fails, and the BEF and French northern forces are now ordered to retreat to Dunkirk to be evacuated.

24 May The XIX Panzerkorps spearheads reach the Aa River, only 25 miles from Dunkirk. Hitler issues a direct order to halt the Panzer advance as the Luftwaffe is given the main role in destroying the Allied northern armies, now retreating to Dunkirk.

25–27 May The German halt order issued for Von Kleist's Panzer forces allows the BEF just enough time to move British units into an effective defence perimeter around Dunkirk.

26 May Operation *Dynamo*, the evacuation of Allied forces from Dunkirk, begins.

26 May–2 June 338,000 British and French soldiers are evacuated from Dunkirk to England. RAF Fighter Command and the Luftwaffe's Luftflotten 2 and 3 plus the VIII Fliegerkorps engage in heavy aerial battles over Dunkirk.

3 June In preparation for *Fall Rot* (Case Red), Luftflotten 2 and 3 carry out an 1,100-aircraft raid on [French] airfields, factories, and military depots in the Paris region. The French air defence performs poorly, with the Luftwaffe losing only four bombers and seven fighters. The 16 airfields and the dozen other targets are hit, with slight to moderate damage, and French air losses amount to about 30 aircraft, including those destroyed on the ground. While inflicting relatively little damage, the massive German air raid deals a psychological blow to the French, showing that the Germans now hold clear air superiority.

5 June *Fall Rot* begins with an offensive by Army Group B, striking out of its bridgeheads on the Somme west of Paris. French Air Force bombers and fighters are thrown into the attack in what will be the busiest day of the French Air Force since the campaign began. Army Group B, with very effective air support from Luftflotte 2, manages to make substantial gains. By 8 June, the French left flank is broken and German forces move rapidly towards the Seine and Paris.

9 June The second phase of *Fall Rot* begins when Gerd von Rundstedt's Army Group A launches its forces, spearheaded by Panzer and motorized divisions, attacking along the Aisne River east of Paris. Again, against a fierce French defence, the main French defensive lines are penetrated in a day, allowing the Germans to move rapidly toward Reims, and into position to envelop Paris. The French air opposition to Von Rundstedt's attack is weak.

10 June With no chance of halting the German advance, the French government decides to leave Paris and set up in Bordeaux. The next day, Paris is declared an open city.

14 June The German Army occupies Paris with no resistance as two German Army groups are moving rapidly into central France.

15 June The French Air Force orders the movement of its most modern aircraft to North Africa, giving France the option of retreating to its North African colonies and continuing the war from there. In the next week, 700–800 French aircraft will be flown to North Africa.

18 June The French government resigns, and a new government headed by World War I hero Marshal Philippe Pétain opens negotiations with the Germans for an armistice to end the fighting.

19 June With the French Army in full retreat, the Luftwaffe's air campaign effectively ends.

22 June France signs an armistice with Germany, ending France's participation in the war.

ATTACKER'S CAPABILITIES
The Luftwaffe

Germany had fielded a large air force in World War I, the *Luftstreitkräfte*, but was forbidden by the Versailles Treaty from having an air force from 1920–35. However, the German Army had maintained an air cadre of hundreds of former Imperial Air Service personnel within the Reichswehr and its general staff. They prepared plans, doctrine, and training, and worked secretly with German civil aviation, which was dominated by former Air Service officers, for the time when Germany would rearm and create a new, modern air force. When Hitler assumed power in January 1933, the plans were put into effect and the Air Ministry (*Luftfahrtministerium*) was created as a supposedly civilian agency, but was actually a Luftwaffe General Staff with talented general staff officers transferred to create a new Luftwaffe, which came into official being in 1935. But already in 1933, the government had poured money into the German aircraft industry, which employed fewer than 3,000 workers at the start of the year, but by year's end employed 11,000 workers building aircraft such as 'fast mail planes' (bombers) and 'sport planes' (fighters) as a means of jump-starting rearmament.

When the Luftwaffe was announced as a full branch of the Wehrmacht in March 1935, it was already a sizeable force. It was created as a multi-purpose air force that would be able to conduct strategic bombing, army support operations, air defence, and even large paratroop and glider operations. In 1935, the Luftwaffe had established its own general staff college to prepare an elite cadre of officers for higher command and staff duties. All mid-ranking officers from all branches (Flying Troops, Flak, Signals, Supply, Engineering) attended a three-month course at the *Luftkreisschule* (Air District School) in Berlin, which centred on doctrine and many wargames and exercises in which the students would plan and execute group and *Geschwader* (Wing-100 aircraft) missions of all types.

By 1939, Germany had the most capable air force in the world and was manufacturing over 10,000 of the most modern military aircraft per year. The Germans had deployed a large air contingent to support the Nationalists in the Spanish Civil War (1936–39), and had gained vast combat experience in modern air war and had also proved a decisive factor in the Nationalist victory.

A Ju 88 medium bomber. One of the best medium bombers to see service during World War II, the Ju 88 was just coming into service with the Luftwaffe in 1940. (AC)

A squadron of Dornier Do 17s on a mission during the campaign in France. The Dornier Do 17 was a fast and very effective light bomber used extensively in that role during the 1940 campaign. Many Dornier Do 17s equipped the long-range reconnaissance flights and squadrons of the Luftwaffe in 1940. (Alamy)

Like other air forces, the Luftwaffe combat aircraft were organized into squadrons with two to four squadrons constituting a group. Above that, the Luftwaffe created the *Fliegerkorps* (Air Corps) to be the operational command for groups, normally of 300–500 aircraft. A Fliegerkorps operated as a permanent headquarters to provide not only command and control for its assigned groups, but also had supporting units including airfield and supply companies, Luftwaffe signals battalions, flak units for air defence, and usually a flight of long-range Do 17 aircraft for long-range reconnaissance. In 1940, the Fliegerkorps tended to be bomber-oriented, consisting of six or more He 111 or Ju 88 medium bomber groups and several groups of Bf 109s or Bf 110s to serve as escort. Other Fliegerkorps were for special purposes. The X Fliegerkorps was a large force organized to support naval operations. The VIII Fliegerkorps was organized as a specialist close air support force equipped with a Dornier Do 17 light bomber group, almost half the Luftwaffe's Stuka and Henschel Hs 123 attack groups, and several fighter groups to provide escort. Two or more Fliegerkorps were typically organized into a *Luftflotte* (Air Fleet), which also constituted a permanent headquarters with its own signals support, supply, and flak units.

Strategic orders for the Luftwaffe were passed down from the High Command in Berlin to army groups and air fleets. From there, they were passed on to the corresponding ground armies and the air corps. While the Luftwaffe was not under army command, the German method was to align air fleets with army groups and air corps, with the specific armies that the air corps were ordered to support. Luftwaffe air corps normally established their forward headquarters next to the headquarters of their army counterparts so that when questions about air support arose, the Fliegerkorps commander or his chief of staff – one of whom was always present at the forward headquarters – could confer with his counterpart army commander or chief of staff, enabling rapid decisions to deploy air units. The Luftwaffe and the army had worked together to plan and conduct air and ground operations since the founding of the Luftwaffe in 1935. While routine in German doctrine and operations, however, this level of combined air-ground planning was unknown to the Allied air forces. Allied joint team operations and planning would not emerge for another two years.

Luftwaffe doctrine

The Luftwaffe published an extensive operational doctrine in 1935 called *Luftkriegsführung*, also known as Luftwaffe Regulation 16 (*Conduct of the Aerial War*). German doctrine was written for the Luftwaffe as a multi-purpose air force, and there was extensive doctrine about conducting strategic air campaigns against enemy industry and key logistics. Luftwaffe doctrine also recognized that success on the battlefield would depend on the Luftwaffe's providing effective support to ground operations. Luftwaffe doctrine contained extensive discussions about key targets, and when and where such targets might be prioritized under particular circumstances. In terms of supporting an army, however, the Luftwaffe doctrine was fairly straightforward. Any air campaign would begin by attacking enemy airfields in a systematic way to win and maintain air superiority as a first priority.

Actual support for army ground operations consisted primarily of Stukas and attack planes (Hs 123s) attacking front-line positions as flying artillery, while light and medium bombers attacked artillery positions, headquarters, supply dumps, and troop concentrations just behind the front lines. Meanwhile, medium bombers would be engaged far to the enemy rear with the primary mission of interdicting rail centres in order to inhibit enemy troop movements. Interdicting troop movements by road was also a major mission of the bombers. As the campaign progressed, with air superiority won, the ground war would become more fluid, and Luftwaffe medium bombers could be employed deep in the enemy rear, attacking factories, ports, and logistics centres.

A key part of the Luftwaffe's command and control system for cooperating with the army was the creation of a specially trained corps of air liaison officers, who would move and operate with the ground forces. These officers, termed *Fliegerverbindungsoffiziere* (Air Liaison Officers) or FLIVOs, were experienced mid-ranking officers with their own communications teams, allowing them to report immediately to the air corps to which they were assigned. FLIVO teams were with each army corps headquarters, and each of the ten Panzer divisions had its own FLIVO team. FLIVO teams ensured that the air corps commanders were fully informed of the air and ground situations along their part of the front. In case of an enemy attack or counteroffensive, the FLIVOs would provide the air corps commander and/or his chief of staff with immediate information, enabling the air corps commander or chief of staff to confer without delay with their army counterparts and order an air mission. Thus, when confronted with an attack or crisis on the ground leading to a call for air support from a Panzer division or army corps, the FLIVOs enabled air commanders to order a response within 45–75 minutes in the form of a Stuka or bomber group, escorted by a fighter group. Neither the BEF nor l'Armée de l'Air was capable of such a quick response to a request for air support.

The creation of specialized ground support units in the Luftwaffe began with Germany's World War I experience. In 1917, the Germans adapted many of their two-seater reconnaissance airplanes for ground attack. For defence against ground fire, armour was mounted around the aircraft engine, and the pilot and observer seats. Armed with three machine guns and able to carry 100kg of bombs, these *Schlachtflieger* (battle planes) constituted 10% of the Imperial Air Force's aircraft by 1918. The Germans found that when used en masse, with two or three squadrons making the attack together, the battle planes could be quite effective against enemy artillery positions and against troops in the open, whether marching to support an attack or reinforcements marching to support a defence.

The Luftwaffe gained a great deal of experience supporting ground operations during

A Heinkel He 111 medium bomber over France in 1940. The He 111 was the Luftwaffe's main medium bomber in the early war years, until replaced by the Ju 88. (Alamy)

the Spanish Civil War, where the Luftwaffe's Condor Legion supported the Nationalist ground armies as their primary mission. As the Nationalists lacked the level of artillery firepower that had been the norm for the combatants on the Western Front, the Condor Legion served as flying artillery, replacing the big guns with bombs from aircraft. The Germans of the Condor Legion, initially equipped with first-generation Heinkel He 51 fighters, found their fighters were inferior in air combat to the Russian-supplied biplane and monoplane fighters equipping the Republican Air Force. So, the

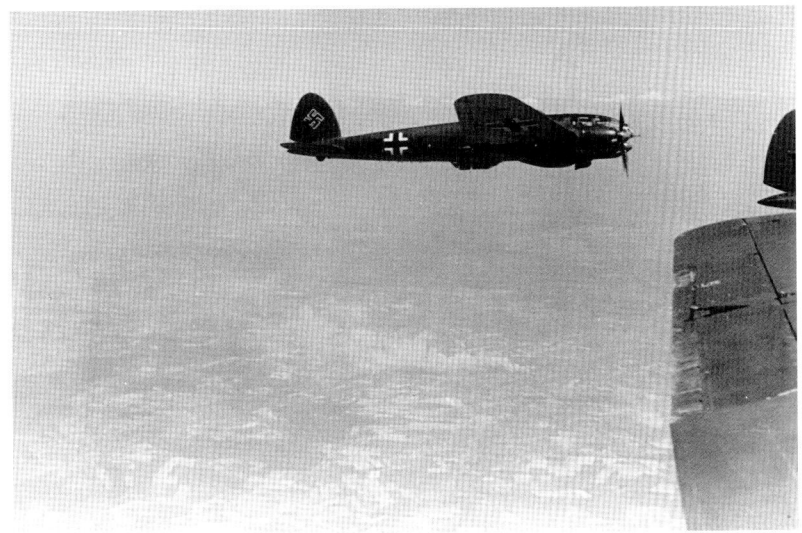

Flight of Bf 110s over France. The Bf 110 was conceived as a long-range heavy fighter plane. With two 1,100hp engines and an armament of two cannon and five machine guns, it could fly at 340mph. It had many good qualities that made it an excellent night fighter, long-range reconnaissance plane, and fighter bomber during the war. However, it was a big disappointment as an air-to-air fighter as its lack of manoeuvrability made it easy for a Hurricane or other fast fighter to best the Bf 110 in a dogfight. (AC)

Condor Legion withdrew its fighters from escort duty, and instead used them in close support operations, dropping bombs and making strafing attacks against the enemy front lines. Condor Legion bombers found that bombing artillery positions, supply points, and reserve troops just behind the front lines was also very effective. The Condor Legion also tested the prototype Ju 87 dive bombers in combat in Spain and found them exceptionally effective for attacking precise targets. Since the 1920s, German operational doctrine had stressed that dive bombers could be very useful weapons not only in close support, but also in attacking point targets with accuracy.

Coming only months after the end of the Spanish Civil War, the Luftwaffe in Poland built on the lessons learned there. A special air division consisting of Stukas, fighters, and light bombers was organized and Generalmajor Wolfram von Richthofen, the last commander of the Condor Legion, was given command, with his priority mission to support the rapid advance of the Panzer divisions. In Poland, the new Luftwaffe doctrine proved highly effective for breaking Polish fortifications, cutting Polish rail lines, and inhibiting Polish troop movements, relentlessly attacking Polish Army formations, and disrupting Polish counterattacks and defensive movements. Another key innovation of the Luftwaffe was to use its large transport force of Ju 52 trimotor transports (each capable of carrying three tons of troops or supplies) as a means of supplying Luftwaffe and Panzer units. The Stukas and Henschels and their accompanying Me 109 escort fighters were all short-range weapons, about 150 miles from their airbase being their maximum operational range. To maintain the offensive, the Luftwaffe had over 100 airfield operations engineers and supply columns, all motorized, that would move directly behind the armoured spearheads and set up temporary forward airfields so that the German fighters and Stukas could move forward as the army advanced. The Luftwaffe's transports could fly personnel, fuel, and munitions to the forward airfields to keep up the tempo of operations. As Stuka and fighter groups typically fly three to five missions per day, the forward airfields enabled them to quickly rearm and refuel their aircraft for the next sortie. As a plus for the army, as the Panzer divisions outran their supply columns, they could maintain their advance with supplies, mostly fuel, flown to temporary airfields close to the front lines.

German commanders

Generaloberst Erhard Milch (1892–1972)

Erhard Milch, who had served as State Secretary for Aviation since 1933, was the man who actually ran the Luftwaffe from the 1930s through World War II. Milch, more than anyone else, had created the Luftwaffe's infrastructure and command system, and had organized the Luftwaffe into the force that it was in 1940.

Reichsmarschall Hermann Göring was officially Commander-in-Chief of the Luftwaffe. Göring, a famous fighter ace in World War I, had last flown an airplane in 1923. Moreover, after World War I, Göring's interests and ambitions had turned from aviation to politics. In the early 1920s, Göring had not only become an early member of the Nazi Party but had also become part of Hitler's inner circle. With his war-hero status and upper-class background, coupled with his personal charm, Göring was the perfect man to represent the Nazis to Germany's ultra-wealthy industrialists and upper classes. So, Hitler had made him his deputy, the number two man in the Third Reich. Göring was incredibly corrupt and had little time or interest in the day-to-day operations and build-up of the Luftwaffe, preferring to spend his time on politics as the Reichsmarschall and Minister-President of the Prussian State.

Göring had engaged in Germany's 1940 offensive only twice, the first being a trip to the just-occupied Netherlands, not to see how air operations were progressing but to look at Dutch art collections to see what he could add to his own immense personal collection. The only other major impact by Göring on the 1940 campaign was to convince Hitler on 23 May 1940 to stop Von Kleist's Panzer advance on Dunkirk, claiming that 'his' Luftwaffe could destroy the British and French armies caught in the huge Flanders pocket by airpower alone. He made this claim without consulting his air fleet commanders, who were appalled at the idea that their forces, having taken heavy losses in the first two weeks of the campaign, were in a condition to carry out Göring's boast. Thus, ironically, Hermann Göring would end up preserving the British Army so that it could rebuild and fight again.

Erhard Milch joined the German Army, was commissioned as an artillery officer in 1910, and served on the Eastern Front in the first months of World War I. In 1915, he joined the Imperial Air Service as an air observer. His leadership qualities were evident, and he was promoted to squadron commander. At the end of the war, he was a captain in command of a fighter group.

Generaloberst Erhard Milch, State Secretary for Aviation (left) and Generalmajor Wolfram von Richthofen, Commander of VIII Fliegerkorps in France, June 1940. (AC)

After the war, Milch turned to a career in civil aviation, founding a small air transport company. By 1925, he was a managing director for Junkers Airlines. When a merger of German airlines occurred in 1926, he became a senior managing director of Lufthansa. Under Milch's management, Lufthansa became a premier European airline. In 1933, Milch, who had maintained his close connections to the German military and was also a staunch supporter of Hitler, was moved into the newly created *Luftfahrtministerium* (Air Ministry), which was nothing more than a disguised Luftwaffe General Staff. As State Secretary for Aviation, Milch was in control of the Luftwaffe budget and expansion, except for aircraft production. From 1933, Milch directed the incredibly rapid growth of the Luftwaffe as it became the world's premier air force by 1939. In terms of airpower, Milch was a highly pragmatic problem-solver. As the Luftwaffe began its expansion, he knew that it would need many modern, all-weather, permanent airfields. So Milch found Germany's top airfield engineer, who was also a professor of engineering, made him a Luftwaffe general, and set him to the task of building hundreds of modern airfields.

Milch had been key to the German victory in Poland by creating a very efficient mobile logistics system that allowed the Luftwaffe to operate its short-range Stukas and fighters from temporary forward airfields. Milch also desired to prove himself as a combat commander, so when Germany invaded Norway on 9 April 1940, Milch took command of all the air operations in the theatre, creating Luftflotte 5 with himself as commander. During his month as air commander for Norway, Milch reorganized his air units into task forces and made sure that captured Norwegian airfields were quickly rebuilt so that the heavier German bombers and Stukas could be based there. By the invasion of France, the Norway campaign was all but over except for continued battles in Norway's far north at Narvik.

Resuming his job as State Secretary for Aviation, Milch visited Luftflotten 2 and 3 and, in his typical problem-solving fashion, cut red tape to ensure replacement pilots and aircraft reached the front in France. Milch ensured that the two air fleets, while still not at full strength, had enough pilots, aircraft, munitions, and fuel to begin the second phase of the 1940 campaign, *Fall Rot*.

A Henschel Hs 126. This two-seater high-wing monoplane served as the short-range reconnaissance and artillery-spotting aircraft for the army corps. More than 300 served under KOLUFT (Kommandeur der Luftwaffe) under army command in the 1940 campaign. In this photo, the observer is taking a photograph. (AC)

Milch was promoted to field marshal after the 1940 campaign and continued to serve as State Secretary for Aviation. In 1941, when the incompetent Ernst Udet, who was responsible for German aircraft production, killed himself, Milch finally took control of aircraft production, which he quickly doubled in a matter of months. Erhard Milch was not particularly liked by the other senior commanders of the Luftwaffe, as he was considered to be too political, but no one in high command could doubt that Milch had truly earned a reputation as a first-rate manager and problem-solver.

General der Flieger Albert Kesselring (1885–1960)

Albert Kesselring, from the Bavarian middle class, joined the Bavarian Army as an artillery officer in 1904. During World War I, Kesselring served on both the Eastern and Western Fronts, and was promoted to captain in 1916. His abilities as a planner and organizer brought him to staff positions at the divisional and army level. In the 1920s, Kesselring served in various staff positions at Reichswehr Headquarters in Berlin, including the Training Branch as well as War Plans. His abilities as a staff officer placed him in the ranks of those mid-level officers who in the future would be likely candidates for army chief of staff.

In 1933, Kesselring's army career was brought to a halt when he was ordered to officially retire and was moved to

General der Flieger Albert Kesselring, Commander of Luftflotte 2. (AC)

the newly established Air Ministry, where he secretly retained his military status as the Air Ministry required a cadre of exceptional staff officers to oversee the development of the Luftwaffe. When he was transferred to the Air Ministry, Kesselring responded like the good soldier and, at age 48, he learned to fly and immersed himself in aviation issues. Kesselring would remain a very avid pilot to the end of his military career.

Kesselring was appointed as a major general in 1934, and a lieutenant general in 1936. His talent as a planner and staff officer was a key factor in the early growth of the Luftwaffe. In June 1936, upon the untimely death of the Luftwaffe's first Chief of Staff Walther Wever in an aircraft accident, Kesselring was made Luftwaffe Chief of Staff. As Chief of Staff, Kesselring served as an advocate for a strong strategic bombing force, and he insisted that the Luftwaffe, which that year rejected two prototype four-engine bomber designs as 'mediocre', would continue to support the development of a heavy four-engine bomber, which turned into the Heinkel He 177 bomber.

After only one year as Luftwaffe Chief of Staff, Kesselring asked to be relieved, largely due to his ongoing conflicts with Erhard Milch. In 1937, he was promoted to General der Flieger and put in command of what was to become Luftflotte 1. In the Polish campaign, Kesselring served with distinction as Luftflotte 1 commander, which included 1,105 aircraft. He conducted the campaign per Luftwaffe doctrine, first targeting all Polish airfields, air factories, and air depots, forcing the Polish Air Force to operate from small auxiliary airfields that lacked adequate supplies of fuel and parts, and then turned to supporting the German Army's ground offensive.

In January 1940, Kesselring was appointed commander of Luftflotte 2. Kesselring commanded Luftflotte 2 throughout the battle for France and the Battle of Britain. Then 1941 saw Kesselring in Russia as the air fleet commander, but in November 1941, with Italy doing very badly in the war, Kesselring was ordered to Italy, where he became Commander-

General der Flieger Hugo Sperrle, Commander of Luftflotte 3. (AC)

in-Chief of Wehrmacht forces in the Mediterranean theatre. Kesselring achieved considerable fame as one of Germany's most capable senior commanders. His effective defence of Italy from 1943 to 1945, carried out with the moderate resources allowed to a secondary theatre of operations, tied up a vast number of Allied troops and resources until the end of the war.

General der Flieger Hugo Sperrle (1885–1953)

Hugo Sperrle, son of a Württemberg brewery owner, began his military career as an artillery lieutenant in 1903. In 1913, having been selected for the elite General Staff College course, Sperrle opted to transfer to the brand-new Imperial Air Service, where he became an aerial observer. During World War I, Sperrle became known as a communications and reconnaissance specialist. By the end of the war, as a captain, Sperrle commanded all the air units of the German 7th Army.

In the interwar period, Sperrle served on the secret air section of the Reichswehr General Staff. In the 1920s, he also served for two years as the senior air officer of the Reichswehr General Staff. Along with other experienced army officers, he was transferred to the Air Ministry in 1934 as a major general and commander of Army Support Aviation. When the Spanish Civil War broke out, Sperrle was appointed as commander of the Luftwaffe's Condor Legion, composed of 5,000 personnel from all branches of the Luftwaffe, supporting a task force of over 100 aircraft. The chief of staff of Sperrle's Condor Legion would be Generalmajor Wolfram von Richthofen; the two made an excellent command team. Sperrle would work primarily at the strategic level with General Franco and the Spanish Nationalist staff, while Von Richthofen planned and directed Condor Legion operations. Under Sperrle and Von Richthofen, the Condor Legion became adept at carrying out all kinds of air operations, including strategic bombing and naval air operations. However, the focus of the Condor Legion was to support the Nationalist Army.

The Spanish Nationalist Army did not have enough artillery to fight a World War I type of war. Thus, the Condor Legion would serve as flying artillery to break the defences of the Spanish Republican forces. When the German Heinkel He 51 fighters sent to the Condor Legion proved to be far inferior to the Soviet-supplied fighter planes sent to the Republic, Sperrle and Von Richthofen converted the obsolete fighters into ground attack aircraft, whereupon they performed very capably in that role. In spring 1937, Sperrle and Von Richthofen patched together an improvised communications net that allowed commanders on the ground to directly observe and communicate with the aircraft attacking front-line positions. This major innovation in air warfare proved to be highly effective. During crises such as the Republic's major offensive at Brunete in 1937, the Condor Legion was given command of the allied Spanish Nationalist and Italian air forces serving in Spain, so that Sperrle ended up in command of up to 300 combat aircraft during campaigns. The Condor Legion proved to be a key element in the ultimate victory of the Spanish Nationalists.

Returning in November 1937 after a year in Spain, Sperrle was appointed to command the Luftwaffe's Third Group, which would become Luftflotte 3. Sperrle passed on the lessons of the Spanish War to the Luftwaffe and his own command. Assuming command of Luftwaffe 3, Sperrle noted that he had lost more aircraft in Spain to accidents under nighttime and bad weather conditions than to combat. His first order to his new command was for all aircraft, especially his bombers, to undergo extensive training and exercises in flying and navigating at night and in bad weather. As a result, the Luftwaffe had far superior skills in night flying and navigation than the French and British air forces, which emphasized strategic bombing but neglected the basic skills necessary to fly missions at night or in overcast weather.

Sperrle proved to be a very capable air commander. In May–June 1940, again per German doctrine, he began the campaign by attacking enemy airfields. Although this did not inflict nearly the damage that he expected, it worked to accelerate the self-imposed logistics problems plaguing l'Armée de l'Air. His overall air campaign was similar to the fighting he had conducted in Spain, with Luftflotte 3's medium bombers carrying out numerous missions deep in the French rear, targeting the French rail network. He also directed bombers and Stukas to support the ground advance, keeping Von Richthofen's VIII Fliegerkorps as a specialist force for close support.

Sperrle commanded Luftflotte 3 in the Battle of Britain and remained as the Luftwaffe's commander on the Western Front until autumn 1944, when owing to overwhelming Allied air superiority, Luftflotte 3, now a totally impotent force, was disbanded. Sperrle was placed on the inactive officers' list and played no further role in the war.

Generalmajor Wolfram von Richthofen (1895–1945)

Wolfram von Richthofen came from Germany's landed aristocracy. His father owned a large estate and his uncle Manfred served as a General der Kavallerie in World War I. Commissioned a lieutenant of cavalry in 1913, he served on the Eastern Front until transferring to the Imperial Air Service in 1917. He was assigned to his famous cousin Manfred's Jagdgeschwader 1 in April 1918. During the 1918 battles, he was credited with eight Allied aircraft.

Wolfram von Richthofen was very technically minded. After World War I, he studied at the Technische Hochschule Hannover, where he attained a degree in engineering in 1922. He was invited to return to the army by German Commander-in-Chief Hans von Seeckt, who wanted to have more technically trained officers on the General Staff. Von Richthofen served on the General Staff's secret air section and continued a programme of study in Berlin, where he attained a PhD in aeronautical engineering. His PhD thesis, which the Reichswehr made top secret, was essentially an industrial rearmament plan discussing the advantages and

A Henschel Hs 123 assault plane. Though obsolete, the Luftwaffe found that this rugged and sturdy biplane was still effective in the close air support role, and a group of Hs 123s served in Von Richthofen's VIII Fliegerkorps throughout the French campaign. (Alamy)

Luftwaffe 88mm heavy flak gun being towed. This gun could be set up quickly and used either in the anti-aircraft role or in direct support of the ground battle. Germans had learned in Spain that the 88mm gun was a superb artillery piece for destroying tanks and fortifications. (AC)

disadvantages of aircraft production methods. Von Richthofen learned Italian and was sent to Italy as an unofficial air attaché in 1929–31.

With the creation of the Luftfahrtministerium in 1933, Von Richthofen was transferred to that organization, where he served as the deputy for the Technical Office, which developed the Luftwaffe's second generation of aircraft, including the Bf 109, the He 111, and the Ju 87 Stuka. In 1936, he had the opportunity of a field command when the Spanish Civil War broke out. In November, he was sent to Spain to serve as Chief of Staff of the Condor Legion under General der Flieger Hugo Sperrle. As Chief of Staff of the Condor Legion, Von Richthofen developed an array of new tactics for ground support, including the use of air-to-ground communications, whereby commanders on the ground could direct aircraft to targets on the front line. He also employed the Condor Legion's large flak contingent directly in the ground battle, proving that Germany's 88mm heavy anti-aircraft gun and the light 20mm and 37mm flak guns were very effective in supporting ground troops. The 88mm flak gun was especially useful for destroying reinforced-concrete bunkers. For the major battles at Bilbao in June 1937 and at Brunete in July 1937, Von Richthofen planned and executed very effective close air support that enabled the Spanish Nationalist Army to break through well-fortified defensive lines. It was a useful lesson that would soon be applied in Poland and in France.

Upon his return from Spain, Von Richthofen served briefly as a bomber wing commander and then from late 1938 to April 1939, he served as the last commander of the Condor Legion. By the start of World War II, Von Richthofen was the Luftwaffe's leading expert in close air support for ground troops. For the Polish campaign he was given a large force, held as a special-purpose air division that included Stukas and light bombers with Bf 109 fighters as escorts, to serve primarily as close air support for the Panzer divisions. After the Polish campaign, Von Richthofen's special air division was expanded and renamed the VIII

Fliegerkorps. As in Poland, Von Richthofen would be engaged in supporting the major Panzer operations in May and June 1940.

During the period of the Phoney War, Von Richthofen kept the VIII Fliegerkorps constantly training and holding exercises for his groups and wings. He also worked at improving Luftwaffe and army communications, which had often proved deficient in Poland. During the Phoney War, he placed his FLIVOs (Air Liaison Officers) in armoured cars with radios so they could observe and control Luftwaffe attacks from the ground. However, this system had not been fully worked out by the start of the campaign, but would be used in June 1941 during the invasion of Russia.

Von Richthofen was Germany's top specialist in close air support for ground troops, but this exceptionally capable officer also showed talent commanding large air forces when he became Luftflotte 4 commander in Russia in 1942. In June 1943, Von Richthofen was transferred to Italy to take command of Luftflotte 2. For the next year and a half, he would work closely with Generalfeldmarschall Albert Kesselring, German Commander-in-Chief in the Mediterranean. Von Richthofen conducted attacks against Allied shipping, but 1943–44 saw the Luftwaffe in Italy in drastic decline. In late 1944, he was diagnosed with a brain tumour and sent to the German military hospital in Bad Ischl, Austria, where he died under American occupation in July 1945.

ORDER OF BATTLE: GERMAN FORCES

HEERESGRUPPE A – GENERALOBERST GERD VON RUNDSTEDT
Gruppe Kleist – General der Kavallerie Ewald von Kleist
XIX Panzerkorps
1. Panzer-Division
2. Panzer-Division
10. Panzer-Division
IR 'Grossdeutschland'
XLI Armeekorps (mot.)
6. Panzer-Division
8. Panzer-Division
2. Infanterie-Division (mot.)
XIV Armeekorps (mot.)
13. Infanterie-Division (mot.)
29. Infanterie-Division (mot.)

AOK 4 – Generaloberst Günther von Kluge
II Armeekorps
12. Infanterie-Division
32. Infanterie-Division
V Armeekorps
251. Infanterie-Division
267. Infanterie-Division
VIII Armeekorps
28. Infanterie-Division

XV Armeekorps (mot.)
5. Panzer-Division
7. Panzer-Division
62. Infanterie-Division
Army Reserve
4. Infanterie-Division
87. Infanterie-Division
211. Infanterie-Division
263. Infanterie-Division

AOK 12 – Generaloberst Siegmund List
III Armeekorps
3. Infanterie-Division
23. Infanterie-Division
VI Armeekorps
16. Infanterie-Division
24. Infanterie-Division
XVIII Armeekorps
5. Infanterie-Division
21. Infanterie-Division
25. Infanterie-Division
1. Gebirgs-Division
Army Reserve
9. Infanterie-Division
27. Infanterie-Division

AOK 16 – General der Infanterie Busch
VII Armeekorps
36. Infanterie-Division
68. Infanterie-Division
XIII Armeekorps
17. Infanterie-Division
34. Infanterie-Division
XXIII Armeekorps
58. Infanterie-Division
76. Infanterie-Division
Army Reserve
6. Infanterie-Division
15. Infanterie-Division
26. Infanterie-Division
33. Infanterie-Division
52. Infanterie-Division
71. Infanterie-Division
73. Infanterie-Division

LUFTWAFFE
LUFTFLOTTE 2: GENERAL DER FLIEGER ALBERT KESSELRING
Aircraft totals: 1,771 Combat Aircraft
Transport Aircraft: 525
Aufklärungsgruppe 122 – Ju 88, He 111
IV Fliegerkorps – General der Flieger Keller
LG 1 – He 111, Ju 88
KG 30 – He 111, Ju 88
KG 27 – He 111
VIII Fliegerkorps – Generalmajor Wolfram von Richthofen
KG 77 – Do 17
StG 2 – Ju 87
StG 77 – Ju 87
JG 27 – Bf 109
Fliegerführer zbV 2 – Generalmajor Putzier
KG 4 – He 111
KG 54 – He 111
Jagdfliegerführer 2 – Oberst von Doring
JG 26 – Bf 109
JG 51 – Bf 109
ZG 26 – Bf 110
7. Fliegerdivision – Generalleutnant Student
Transport Units
KGzbV 1 – 208 Ju 52
KGzbV 2 – 204 Ju 52
KGrzbV 5 – 48 Ju 52, 50 DFS 230
Sonderstaffel: He 59
II Flakkorps
Flak BDE III
Flak Rgt 6
Flak Rgt 8
Flak Rgt 201
Flak Rgt 202

Luftflotte 3 – General der Flieger Hugo Sperrle
Combat Aircraft: 1,756
I Fliegerkorps – General der Flieger Ulrich Grauert
JG 77 – Bf 109
JG 3 – Bf 109
ZG 76 – Bf 110
KG 1 – He 111
KG 76 – Do 17
III/StG 51 – Ju 87
5 (F) 122 – Do 17
II Fliegerkorps – Generalleutnant Bruno Loerzer
KG 2 – Do 17
KG 3 – Do 17
KG 53 – He 111
StG 1 – Ju 87
3(F) 121 – Do 17
V Fliegerkorps – Generalleutnant Robert Ritter von Greim
JG 52 – Bf 109
JG 54 – Bf 109
V (Z) LG 1 – Bf 110
I/ZG 52 – Bf 110
KG 51 – He 111, Ju 88
KG 55 – He 111
4 (F) 121 – Ju 88, Do 17
Jagdfliegerführer 3 – Oberst Gerd von Massow
JG 2 – Bf 109
JG 53 – Bf 109
ZG 2 – Bf 110
I Flakkorps – General der Flakartillerie Hubert Weise
I Flak BDE
Flak Rgt 102
Flak Rgt 103
II Flak BDE
Flak Rgt 101
Flak Rgt 104

KOLUFT
HEERESGRUPPE A
14 Squadrons Hs 126
6 Flights Do 17
HEERESGRUPPE B
9 Squadrons Hs 126
3 Flights Do 17
HEERESGRUPPE C
4 Squadrons Hs 126
4 Flights Do 17

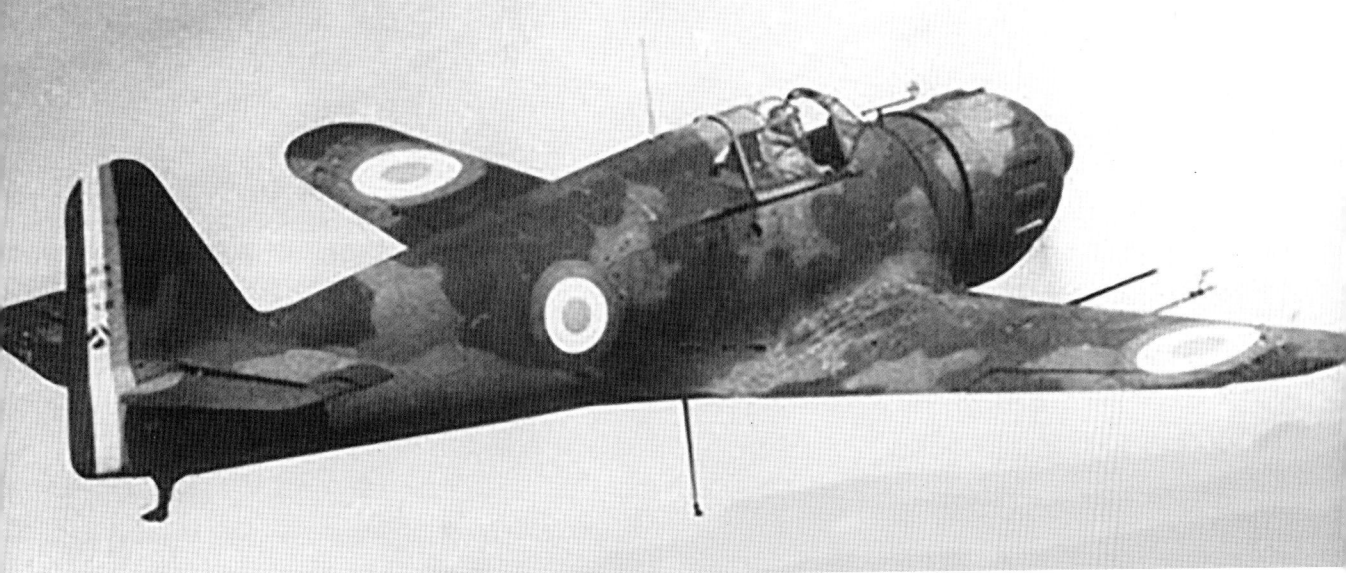

DEFENDER'S CAPABILITIES

Anglo-French airpower

L'Armée de l'Air

By the end of World War I, France was a leading air power with the world's largest aircraft industry. French air technology also led the world and in 1918 French aeronautical engineers produced the first supercharged engine. France was also a leader in developing air combat doctrine. But the French Air Force and the French aviation industry languished in the 1920s and in aviation technology France was quickly surpassed by America, Britain, and Germany.

The commanders of the French Army in the interwar period, Marshal Philippe Pétain in the 1920s and then General Maurice Gamelin in the 1930s, had proved themselves to be outstanding commanders in World War I, but their thinking on aviation, and on war in general, remained fundamentally that of 1918. The military policy for France was crafted around the Conseil Supérieur de la Guerre (CSG), the Superior War Council of the French Armed Forces, which was dominated overwhelmingly by the French Army, and the thinking was overwhelmingly defensive. Therefore, France poured its defence budget into the Maginot Line and spent a far smaller portion of the defence budget on its air force than Britain and Germany during the rearmament of the 1930s.

The French Air Force only became an independent air force in January 1933, but remained subordinate to the Supreme War Council, with the army insisting that the primary duty of the French Air Force was to support the army. However, the newly independent French Air Force had, at the top, officers who were enthralled by the strategic bombing concepts of Italian airpower theorist General Giulio Douhet, who argued that a large fleet of strategic bombers attacking the enemy's homeland and cities could paralyze an enemy nation and cause the enemy to collapse in a matter of weeks, thereby avoiding the massive bloodletting on the ground that France had experienced from 1914 to 1918. Thus, in 1932, the French Air Force had been reequipped with new aircraft that would mostly be bombers. While the army prioritized reconnaissance aircraft and insisted that the air force serve mainly the army support function, the French Air Ministry proposed a new series of aircraft that would meet the army's requirements for reconnaissance and ground attack but would also serve

A French Air Force Bloch MB.152 fighter. The all-metal MB.152 was heavily armed with cannon and machine guns. Its sturdy construction and radial engine would have made it a highly effective ground attack aircraft. As a fighter, however, it was outclassed by the Bf 109 due to the MB.152's slower speed and lesser manoeuvrability. (AC)

A French Bloch MB.131 bomber at Lille, spring 1940. A 1933 design, the MB.131 had a four-man crew. The MB.131 equipped six reconnaissance groups of the French Air Force in France in 1940. Its slow speed (maximum 217mph) and small bombload of only 440lb meant that the Bloch MB.131 could not be effective as a reconnaissance aircraft, so it was used as a night bomber. (IWM)

as long-range strategic bombers able to strike the enemy homeland. What emerged from the French Air Ministry was the Bomber-Combat-Reconnaissance or BCR aircraft. The airplanes developed would be general-purpose aircraft that could serve in all roles, with enough defensive armament to also carry out bombing missions without an escort.

The BCR aircraft produced under the 1934 budget, designed to fill the bombing, ground attack, and reconnaissance roles, were ungainly, underpowered, slow, and – as with aircraft designed to carry out several different missions – thoroughly mediocre at each of them. The Amiot 143 and the Bloch MB. 200 aircraft as well as the Potez 540, built as a bomber as well as a reconnaissance and attack aircraft, were obsolete the day they were built. Unfortunately for the French, the BCR aircraft based on early 1930s designs would tie up the French aircraft industry until 1937.

Meanwhile, the French aircraft industry had fallen far behind. By the mid-1930s, Germany, Britain, and America had developed reliable large aircraft engines producing 1,000+hp to power new all-metal aircraft designs. French industry was unable to mass-produce reliable large engines. So, new French designs of the 1930s were all powered by engines in the 600–800hp range, and almost all the French aircraft were underpowered and were slower and less capable than their counterpart fighters and bombers of the German and British air forces. The French government, knowing it was already far behind the Germans, nationalized the aircraft industry in 1936, but this led to a couple of years of confusion, and by 1937 the French aviation industry was so far behind in production capability that many of the BCR aircraft which l'Armée de l'Air wanted quickly ended up being delivered two years late.

Accordingly, in 1937, the French Air Ministry turned to the idea of purchasing aircraft from the United States. That year, a mission from the French Air Force came to the United States to talk to aviation companies and look to the Americans to manufacture modern fighters and light bombers for the French. It was a decision taken in desperation, as the French would have to spend large sums on foreign aircraft. In 1938, the French agreed to buy an initial purchase of 100 P-36 Hawk fighters, that being the most modern fighter aircraft being built in the United States by the Curtiss Company, with more orders to follow. France also negotiated with the United States to buy the new Martin 167 and Douglas D 7 light bombers, first-rate airplanes that were fully equal to the Luftwaffe's latest aircraft.

By 1938, French industry was developing some good designs, such as the Morane-Saulnier M.S.406, Bloch MB. 152, and Dewoitine D.520 fighters and the Potez 63 heavy fighter and the Lioré et Olivier LeO 45 bomber, but the Bloch, Morane, and Potez fighters were all underpowered and inferior to their German counterparts. Aircraft production levels were half of the output expected, so aircraft like the Dewoitine D.520 would not be available until after the battle for France began.

The personnel situation of the French Air Force was in a disastrous state when General Vuillemin became Air Force Chief of Staff in February 1938. In contrast to Germany and Britain, the army and air force of France's Third Republic traditionally failed to value the professional NCO corps that carried out the technical and specialist supply duties of the French Air Force. The low pay and low living standards for professional NCOs in the French Air Force provided little incentive for bright non-pilots to join the air force. When the war began in 1939, the French Air Force had only 30% of the NCO mechanics required to supervise aircraft maintenance and repair, as well as only 30% of the expert radio NCOs

A Douglas D-7 light bomber. France ordered 270 of these excellent, fast and manoeuvrable light bombers from the United States, but due to the French Air Force's poorly functioning logistics system, only a few managed to fly in combat before France's surrender. The Douglas D-7, also known to the British as the Boston and to the Americans as the A-20 Havoc, was produced in large numbers and served very effectively. (Alamy)

required by its Table of Organization. This meant that a French Air Force senior NCO mechanic stationed at an air depot received far less pay than the junior civilian mechanics that he was supervising.

Neither French Air Force Chief of Staff Vuillemin and Air Minister La Chambre showed any inclination to deal with recruiting, training, or retaining specialist NCO mechanics, armorers, supply specialists, or communications specialists, the very people who ensured that aircraft were maintained, and repaired, and saw that replacement parts and aircraft flowed smoothly. Even in peacetime, French Air Force squadrons typically had a 40%–60% serviceability rate for aircraft on hand, while British and German air units typically had a serviceability rate of more than 80% of assigned aircraft. Low serviceability in wartime was a path to failure.

Adding to the dysfunction of French Air Force logistics was its depot system, in which flyable aircraft were produced and tested at the factory and accepted by the air force, which would then send them to an air depot to receive armament, radios, gunsights, bombsights, and bomb release gear. Owing to a drastic shortage of qualified NCO technicians, the aircraft repair and modification backlog at the air depots was enormous. Due to a poor supply system, there was a shortage of bombsights, instruments, radios, and even machine guns and cannon at the air depots, so that brand-new, flyable aircraft sat at depots for weeks before being equipped for combat operations. In the case of the more than 200 excellent, modern Martin and Douglas light bombers shipped to France in 1939–40, only a few saw action while dozens of aircraft remained on French airfields, awaiting basic equipment such as bombsights.

General Joseph Vuillemin, Chief of Staff of the French Air Force in 1938–40. (Alamy)

The French Air Force's organization was largely a holdover of World War I. A large part of l'Armée de l'Air was assigned to the army operations squadrons and groups assigned to direct army command and control. Each French army was allocated reconnaissance squadrons and fighter squadrons that operated under army command to support each specific army. The remaining French combat aircraft were assigned to air force regional commands. At the outset of the war, the French Air Force established the Zone of Air Operations North (ZOAN), which would operate in support of General Alphonse Joseph Georges's northern group of armies, which included General Billotte's First Army Group as well as eight divisions of the BEF. Other operational zones included ZOAE, Zone of Air Operations East, which commanded air units along France's eastern border covering the Maginot Line. There was also the Zone of Air Operations Alps (ZOAA) and Zone of Air Operations South

OPPOSITE FRENCH AIR BASES 1940

A French Amiot 143 bomber, a product of the early 1930s BCR Programme. This twin-engine bomber with a five-man crew could carry 3,600lb of bombs and had four 7.5mm machine guns for defence. Overweight and underpowered, its maximum speed was 183mph. Although totally obsolete by 1940, l'Armée de l'Air had 87 of these bombers in service, used primarily as night bombers. But in the desperation of the moment, it was used as a day bomber as well as to strike the German bridgehead at Sedan on 14 May 1940. (Alamy)

(ZOAS), which covered France's border with Italy. However, the focus of the main combatant command was ZOAN, commanded by General François d'Astier de La Vigerie, who was allocated more than 500 aircraft. The French Air Force also maintained a special command focused on the air defence of Paris. A large part of the French bomber force consisted of obsolete Farman, Bloch, and Amiot bombers from the BCR program, organized into groups and wings and held as a strategic reserve.

France had little in the way of a modern air doctrine. In 1936, French Air Minister Pierre Cot issued a new air doctrine declaring the priority mission of the air force to be support of the army. But how this might be done, however, was never explained. Some French senior airmen, notably General Aubé, argued for setting up a ground attack force, called assault aviation, in the French Air Force. General Aubé wanted to copy the German ground attack methods that had proved so very effective in Spain. He found some support for his ideas from the Air Ministry, but little progress was made in creating such a force by the time the war had started. However, it was hoped that when enough Potez 63 twin-engine heavy fighters became available, this would be the best aircraft for such a force.

The French Army's anti-aircraft forces were small and obsolete. At the outbreak of war France could mobilize only 2,600 anti-aircraft guns for the defence of the whole country. Most of these were unmodified obsolete World War I 75mm guns, although some of the old guns had been upgraded in the 1920s. But in 1940, the French heavy anti-aircraft guns were obsolete and posed little threat to German bombers flying at high altitude. In the 1930s, the French developed a good Hotchkiss 25mm rapid-fire cannon for low-altitude anti-aircraft defence, but only 500 were available in May 1940 and, of these, only 192 to protect French airfields. France also used the effective 20mm Oerlikon anti-aircraft gun, but only a few hundred were available in 1940.

Because defending cities was a high priority, French Tables of Organization allotted a single light anti-aircraft battery to French armoured and mechanized divisions, but due to the gun shortage not all of those units received even this single battery. French corps and armies typically had few anti-aircraft guns, and there were few light anti-aircraft guns to defend airfields, a prime target for the German Air Force.

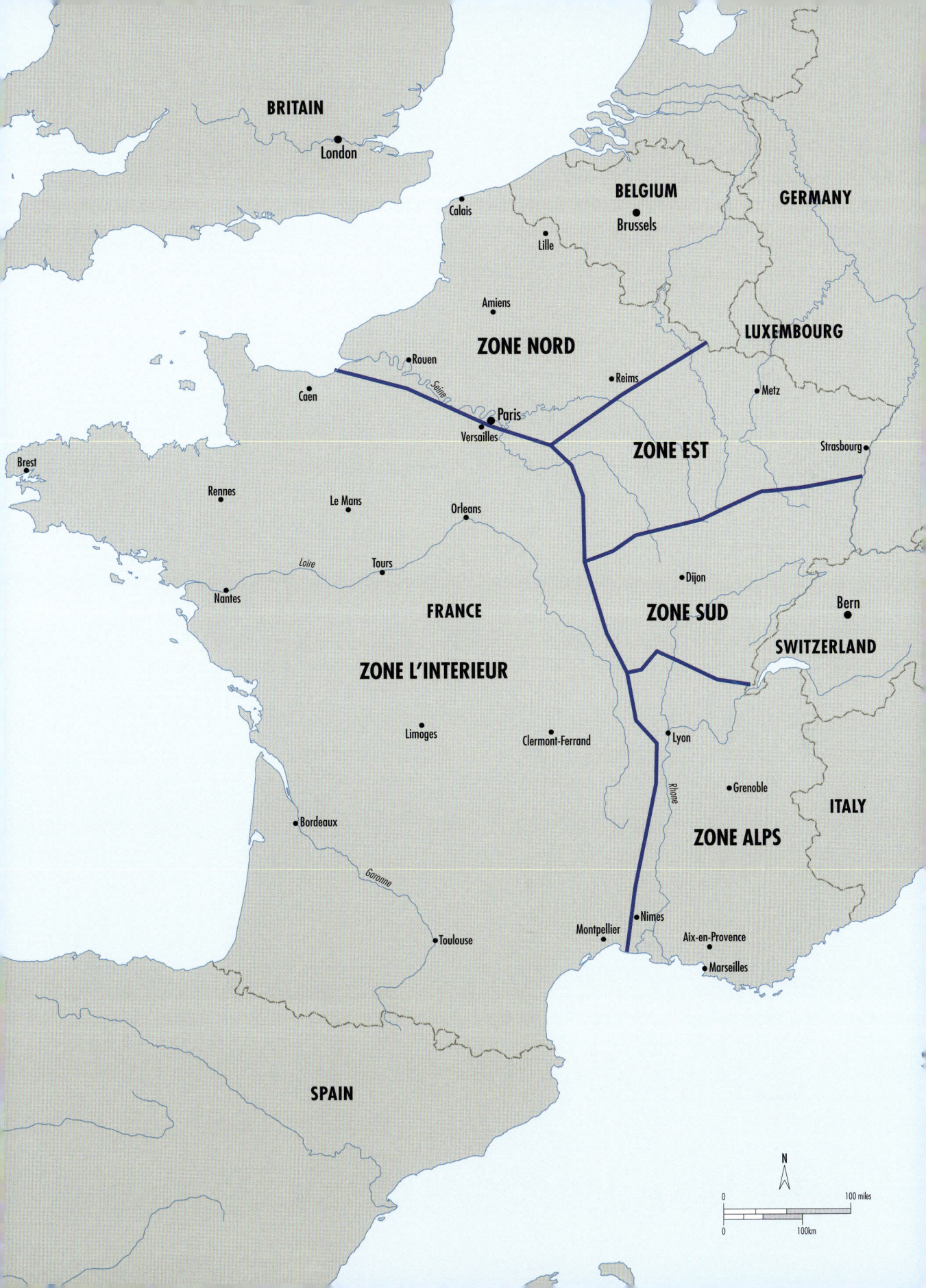

Basically, l'Armée de l'Air in 1940 had few strengths and many fatal weaknesses. The American aircraft purchases had helped solve the problem of aircraft numbers, but other problems such as the lack of technical personnel, the dysfunctional logistics system, and the fragmented command and control could have been dealt with and readily solved if the top military and air leaders had addressed them.

The Royal Air Force

The Royal Air Force (RAF) was created from the Royal Flying Corps (RFC) in 1918. For the first 12 years of its existence, the RAF was dominated by Air Chief Marshal Hugh Trenchard, who had commanded the RFC in France from 1915 to 1918, then had commanded Britain's independent bomber force of heavy bombers in the last year of the war. From 1919 to 1930, he served as Chief of Staff of the RAF.

Trenchard was a firm believer that the strategic bomber, used in a bombing offensive against the enemy homeland and its industries, would be a decisive weapon in winning a future war. The interwar RAF was imbued with strategic bombing theory, which became the core doctrine of the RAF. The other priority of the RAF was the air defence of Great Britain, which was a priority of the British government since the Germans had turned to heavy bombers and bombed England in 1917–18.

While busy in colonial air operations in the interwar period, Trenchard laid a firm foundation for the RAF as a cadre force that could be dramatically and efficiently expanded. In the 1920s, the RAF created the auxiliary squadrons, essentially RAF reserve units staffed with short-service pilots who had undergone RAF pilot training and then served with the auxiliary squadrons. Trenchard also created a school system for the RAF and established the RAF Staff College at Andover, at which selected mid-rank officers would get a thorough education in air operations and strategy. Just as important, Trenchard ensured that the small peacetime air force was well-manned at every level. A bright and ambitious young Briton could join the RAF and receive a first-class technical education as an air force mechanic or armorer or signaller. Good pay, housing, and benefits ensured that becoming an enlisted man in the regular air force was an attractive career. Thus, the RAF possessed highly capable ground crew, mechanics, and support personnel who were responsible for keeping the planes flying.

From the mid-1930s, when the threat of Nazi Germany became evident, Britain embarked on a major rearmament program, with the RAF a major beneficiary of rearmament funding. In the mid-1930s, as well as funding an array of twin-engine medium bombers including the Vickers Wellington, the Armstrong Whitworth Whitley, and the Handley Page Hampden, the

A Lysander Mk. II of No. 13 Squadron RAF in France, winter 1940. The Lysander was designed as an army cooperation aircraft, useful for short-range reconnaissance, liaison, and artillery spotting. This slow but rugged aircraft could operate from small, rough airfields. It was armed with two forward-firing .303 machine guns and two machine guns facing the rear for the observer. It could also carry a 500lb bombload. Though not intended to be used as a bomber, Lysanders were operated in May 1940 by the RAF against German columns. (IWM)

RAF also developed the smaller, twin-engine Blenheim and the single-engine Fairey Battle light bombers, both of which might have been suitable for tactical support but were actually intended to serve in Bomber Command as part of a strategic force. In the mid-1930s, the RAF began development of true, long-range, four-engine bombers capable of carrying large bombloads deep into the enemy homeland. From this initiative initially came the Short Stirling. Then came the Handley Page Halifax heavy bomber, first deployed in 1941. Finally, the Lancaster heavy bomber was deployed for the first time in 1942 and would become the main strategic bomber of Britain.

Though the RAF had not wanted to spend large sums on fighters, under political pressure it had to agree to large-scale production of the Hurricane and Spitfire prototypes, designed around the 1,000+ horsepower Rolls-Royce Merlin engine. In 1936, the RAF was reorganized into specialist commands including a Training Command. Coastal Command was created to support the Royal Navy by conducting anti-shipping operations from Britain. Fighter Command was responsible for the air defence of Britain. Bomber Command was the RAF's priority command for personnel, funding, and doctrine.

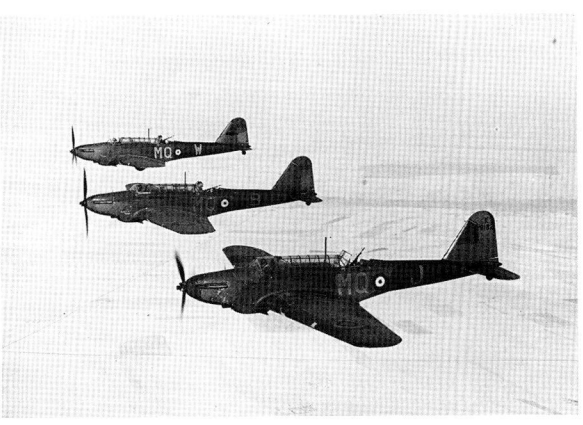

Three Fairey Battle Mk. Is of RAF No. 226 Squadron based in Reims, winter 1940. The Battle was intended by Bomber Command to serve as a strategic bomber, with exceptional long range for a single-engine aircraft. During May 1940, the Battle was employed as a light bomber with a 1,000lb bombload against key targets. Its slow speed, lack of self-sealing fuel tanks, or armour made the Battle exceptionally vulnerable to German flak fire or fighters. The poor performance and heavy losses of the Battle squadrons in May 1940 caused the RAF to take this aircraft out of service. (IWM)

Within the RAF Air Staff, there was little interest in specialized aviation to support the British Army. Army cooperation, for the RAF, meant light aircraft that could operate from small, temporary airfields to provide the ground forces with short-range reconnaissance, artillery-spotting, and liaison. This role was fulfilled by the small, two-seater Westland Lysander aircraft.

While the RAF had aircraft that were suitable for ground attack operations in the Blenheim and Battle light bombers, there was little interest in adapting the Battle into a ground attack plane. Overall, the RAF Air Staff was sceptical about the idea of employing bombers in direct support of ground armies. Furthermore, they saw little need to worry about the issue. Any British ground army on the continent would be relatively small and merely an addition to the French Army. The British government and military had complete faith that the French could handily stop and hold any German Army attack with the Maginot Line and the large force of tanks and artillery that the French Army had at its disposal. Thus, based on this assumption of French prowess, the RAF reasoned that there would be little need to employ bombers in a tactical role against the Germans.

The British Air Forces in France (BAFF)

At the outbreak of war in September 1939, the British Army had already planned with the French to initially send a British army of eight divisions, which would soon be expanded into a larger force. The BEF would constitute a part of the northern group of armies along the French border with Belgium. The RAF would send two different components to France. The main part was the AASF or Advanced Air Striking Force, under the command of Air Vice Marshal Patrick Playfair, consisting of Fairey Battle squadrons, Blenheim squadrons, and three Hurricane fighter squadrons for defending the airfields and for bomber escorts. The second part of the RAF deployed to France was the BEF Air Component, under the command of General Lord Gort, consisting of Blenheim light bomber squadrons, RAF fighter squadrons, and Lysander army cooperation squadrons.

Having two essentially separate RAF commands in France made command and control somewhat difficult, so that in January 1940, Air Marshal Barratt was appointed commander of the British Air Forces France (BAFF), and would have tactical control of the AASF squadrons, but also was expected to coordinate their use with the RAF Bomber Command.

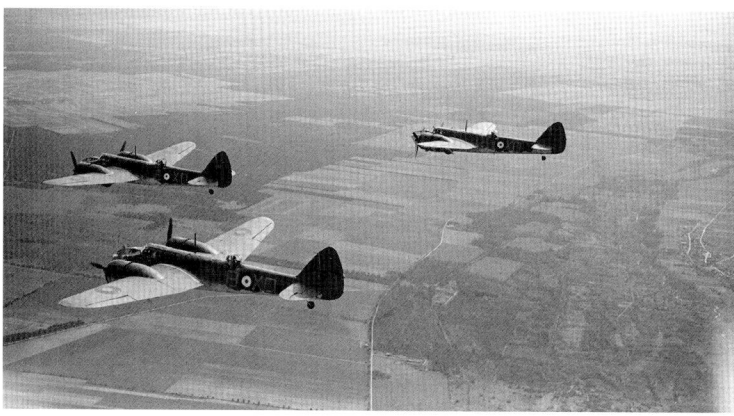

Three Bristol Blenheim Mk. IV bombers of RAF No. 139 Squadron on a reconnaissance mission over northern France in 1940. The Bristol Blenheim came into RAF service in 1937 as a light bomber. It was the RAF's primary light bomber in the early part of the war. It had a maximum speed of 266mph and defensive armament of four .303 machine guns and could carry 1,200lb of bombs. A first-rate light bomber, yet when introduced in 1940, it was already becoming obsolescent. But the Blenheim units saw extensive combat and took heavy losses in May 1940. (IWM)

During the eight months of the 'Phoney War', there was little urgency within the BAFF to develop new doctrine or tactics for the major clash with the German Army and Luftwaffe that was likely to come in the spring. Air Vice Marshal Playfair did look at the likelihood of using the Battle light bombers in a ground attack role, and he had the Battle squadrons conduct exercises for flying low, 50–100ft in altitude, and to practise for attacking German ground columns. Playfair also discussed with the Air Staff the possibility of modifying the Fairey Battles for low-level attack operations. But turning the Fairey Battle into a tactical bomber would require removing the navigator, the autopilot, and large fuel tank located in the fuselage in order to reduce the weight and allow armour and additional machine guns to be installed. However, the Air Staff balked at the idea of modifying the Fairey Battles to create what might have made an adequate low-level attack plane, since keeping them in their current configuration rather than removing the large fuel tank would help the Battles maintain the necessary range to strike well into Germany. The commitment of the RAF staff to strategic bombing was so strong that few questioned how a slow, single-engine bomber with a bombload of only 1,000lb could meaningfully contribute to the destruction of German industry.

With only three Hurricane squadrons to support the dozen bomber squadrons of the AASF, Air Marshal Playfair requested more fighter squadrons. In the meantime, he would look to the French Air Force to provide fighters. The French Air Force commander on the northern front, General d'Astier, agreed that he would provide the AASF with whatever fighter support he could for escort duties. Both the French Air Force and the BAFF were concerned about the dearth of available fighter squadrons, should the Germans attack, as there were simply not enough fighters to defend the French and British airbases, to fly patrols, and keep German bombers away from the ground armies, or to provide escorts for bomber missions.

There were other concerns as well, as both Britain and France were very thin in terms of modern anti-aircraft guns to defend their airfields. The British Army sent two brigades of anti-aircraft guns to support the BEF and the RAF in France. The British Army had adopted the 40mm Bofors anti-aircraft gun, which was an excellent air defence gun against low-altitude aircraft. For work against high-altitude enemy aircraft, the British had recently fielded an excellent 3.7in. heavy anti-aircraft gun with a performance roughly comparable to the German 88mm gun. However, modern heavy anti-aircraft guns were in very short supply, so most of the heavy anti-aircraft guns deployed to the BEF and BAFF were 3in. anti-aircraft guns that were essentially World War I-surplus weapons, and not exceptionally lethal.

Air Marshal Barratt was given vague instructions and assurances by the Air Staff that, if he requested it, then Bomber Command could provide bombers for support missions. Yet at the same time, the Air Staff cautioned Barratt that using bombers in front-line operations, where the German enemy would have plenty of anti-aircraft guns and fighters, would likely lead to unacceptable losses, and that such missions were not worth it.

Allied commanders
General Maurice Gamelin (1872–1958)
For his whole military career, Maurice Gamelin was viewed as a brilliant military intellectual. Gamelin was first in his class of 1893 at Saint-Cyr, the French officer academy. As a young

A French Morane-Saulnier M.S.406, shown here in spring 1940 with Polish insignia, meant to equip Polish fighter squadrons. The M.S.406 went into production in 1938, and more than a thousand were delivered to the French Air Force. It was the most numerous fighter plane for France in 1940. The M.S.406 was France's great hope to match the Bf 109. However, the underpowered M.S.406 had a max speed of only 281mph at 6,000ft and could only reach 300mph at 15,000ft. The M.S.406 was lightly armed with only one 20mm cannon and two 7.5mm machine guns. In speed, armament, and manoeuvrability, it was completely outclassed by the Bf 109. Hundreds of M.S.406s were not available for combat in 1940 because they were languishing in French Air Force depots being slowly modified with a larger engine. (AC)

lieutenant, he served in operations in the French colonies. In 1897, Gamelin was selected to attend the French Army Staff College, the École supérieure de guerre, where he was second in a class of 80 officers. In 1906, Gamelin published *A Philosophical Study on the Art of War*, which received positive reviews and marked him as an officer whose career was on a bright path.

Gamelin was an infantry battalion commander at the start of World War I. By 1916, he was promoted to colonel. In 1917, he was made a general and served as a divisional commander to the end of the war. He earned a reputation as an excellent tactician and operational commander. Gamelin was favoured by Army Chief of Staff General Philippe Pétain, moving up through higher commands to become Chief of Staff of the French Army in 1932. At the outbreak of World War II, Gamelin served as Commander-in-Chief of the French Armed Forces, which meant that he had command over the army and the air force, but not the navy. As France's senior military commander, he chaired the military-civilian Conseil Supérieur de la Guerre (CSG), France's Supreme War Council. The British and French governments would jointly conduct the strategic leadership of the two great empires. As France's ally, Britain committed the BEF to serving in France under French command, so that Gamelin also assumed the chairmanship of the Allied Supreme War Council. More than any other person, Gamelin was responsible for shaping the British and French war strategy against the Germans. The Allied strategy to oppose a German offensive in the Low Countries was Gamelin's strategy, which would fail spectacularly in the 1940 campaign.

Despite his reputation as a thinking general, in fact Gamelin had scarcely changed his understanding of warfare since World War I. With the enormously expensive Maginot Line protecting France's border with Germany, Gamelin believed that France was safe from a German ground attack. However, the French also developed their own tank and mechanized forces and in 1940 the French fielded more, and better, tanks than the German Army. Yet the French approach to armoured warfare was dramatically different from the German approach. German Panzer divisions were balanced, all-arms organizations fielding as many infantry battalions as tank battalions in their organization. Panzer divisions also included motorized artillery battalions, a large engineer battalion, and a full complement of signals and support troops, and as such were capable of independent operations. The French armoured forces, notably the four new armoured divisions being created in 1940,

OPPOSITE FRENCH ZONE NORD (INCLUDES RAF BASES)

were tank-heavy organizations, each including only a small infantry unit, a small artillery battalion, and only one company of engineers. French armour was to be used to break through enemy defences, with infantry divisions following, a doctrine modelled on the successful 1918 offensives. Along with a powerful tank arm, the French Army also possessed a large heavy artillery arm. In May 1940, the French Army fielded twice as many artillery pieces as its German attackers.

Gamelin's understanding of military airpower seems to have been rooted in the doctrines of World War I. In practice, this meant that the air force's job was to serve under army commanders, as in World War I, and provide accurate reconnaissance and fighter aviation to ensure that the enemy air forces were kept away. Gamelin had little use for strategic bombing theories. For him, it was the ground war that mattered, and firepower in the ground war was delivered by artillery, not airpower.

Gamelin was also aware of Germany's bomber forces. During the entire period of the 'Phoney War' from September 1939 to May 1940, Gamelin, supported by his Air Force Chief General Joseph Vuillemin, vetoed every suggestion that the British or French air forces should bomb Germany's industrial Ruhr, as the French feared that the Germans would retaliate with far more powerful bomber attacks against France's cities.

At the start of the war, Gamelin set up his own personal headquarters in the Château de Vincennes, on the edge of Paris. By being close to Paris, he and his small staff of 50 officers remained very close to the government. Gamelin met only rarely with senior air commanders From the Château de Vincennes, and directed the French war effort through telephone and motorcycle dispatch riders. There was no radio communications centre set up for the Supreme Allied Commander.

When the entire Allied strategy for the Low Countries collapsed within four days of the start of the campaign, Gamelin had no alternate plans ready in case the Dyle Plan failed.

General Maurice Gamelin in Paris (second from right) with (left to right) General Field Marshal William Edmund Ironside, 1st Baron Ironside, Chief of the Imperial General Staff; Winston Churchill; and General Lord Gort, Commander of the BEF. Gamelin chaired the Supreme Allied War Council and was there as the senior Allied commander of the 1940 campaign. (IWM)

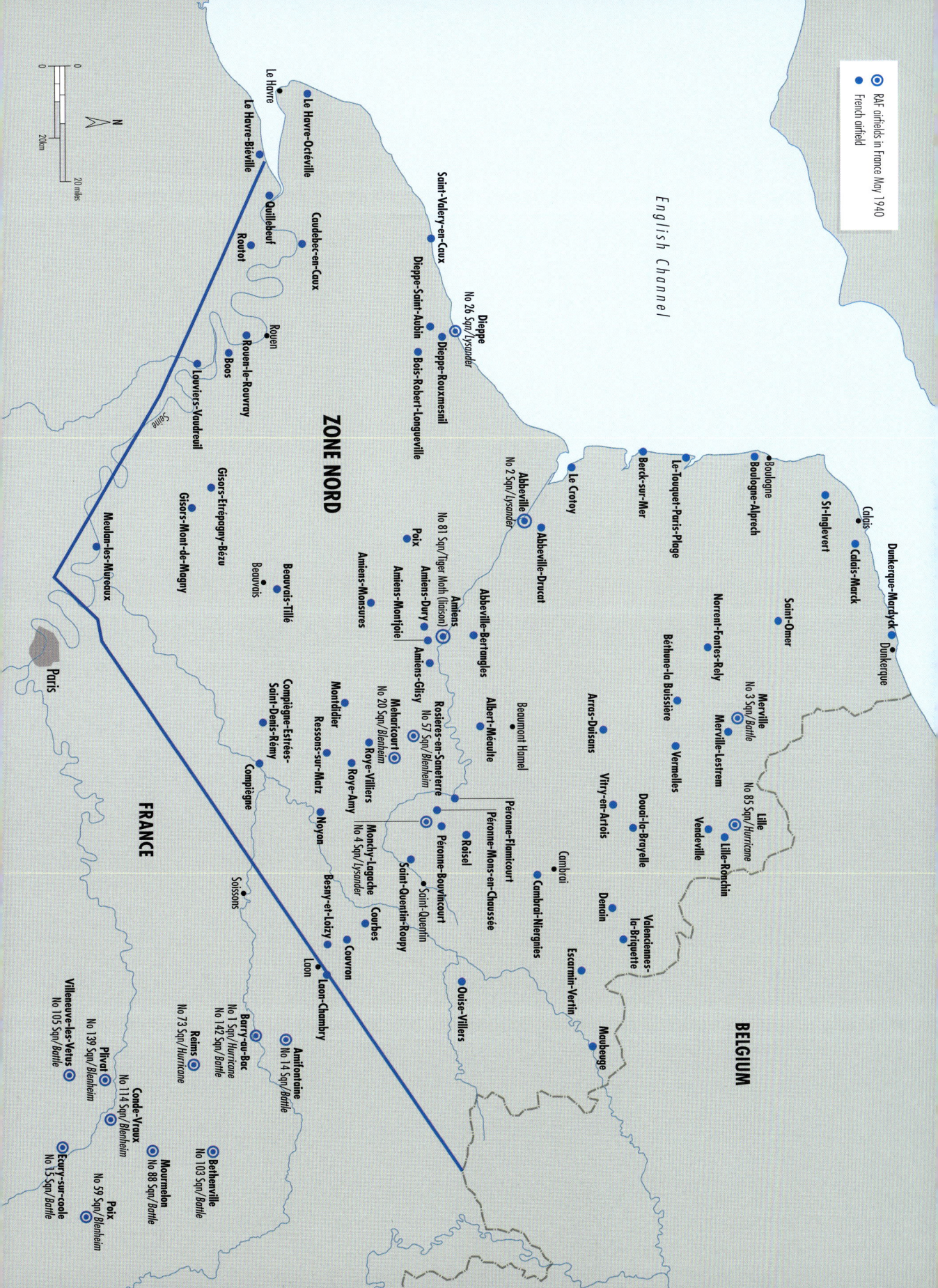

RAF airfields in France May 1940
French airfield

English Channel

N

0 — 20km
0 — 20 miles

Le Havre
Le Havre-Bréville
Quillebeuf
Rouot
Caudebec-en-Caux
Rouen
Boos
Louviers-Vaudreuil
Gisors-Étrépagny-Bézu
Gisors-Mont-de-Magny
Meulan-les-Mureaux

Paris

FRANCE

ZONE NORD

Seine

Le Havre-Octeville
Saint-Valéry-en-Caux
Dieppe-Saint-Aubin
Dieppe-Rouxmesnil
Bois-Robert-Longueville
Rouen-le-Rouvray

Dieppe
No 26 Sqn/Lysander

Le Crotoy

Abbeville
No 2 Sqn/Lysander

Abbeville-Drucat
No 81 Sqn/Tiger Moth (liaison)
Poix
Beauvais-Tillé
Beauvais
Amiens-Monsures
Amiens-Montjoie
Amiens-Dury
Amiens-Glisy
Amiens
Abbeville-Bertangles

Montdidier
Compiègne-Estrées-Saint-Denis-Rémy
Ressons-sur-Matz
Compiègne
Mesnicourt
No 57 Sqn/Blenheim
Rosières-en-Santerre
No 20 Sqn/Blenheim
Roye-Villiers
Roye-Amy
Noyon

Soissons

Berck-sur-Mer
Le Touquet-Paris-Plage
Boulogne
Boulogne-Alprech
St-Inglevert
Calais
Calais-Marck
Dunkerque-Mardyck
Dunkerque

Norrent-Fontes-Rely
Béthune-la-Buissière
Saint-Omer
Merville
No 3 Sqn/Battle
Merville-Lestrem
Vermelles
Arras-Duisans
Vitry-en-Artois
Lille
No 85 Sqn/Hurricane
Lille-Ronchin
Lille-Seclin
Vendeville
Douai-la-Brayelle
Valenciennes-la-Briquette
Escarmin-Vertin
Maubeuge

Beaumont Hamel
Albert-Méaulte
Péronne-Flamicourt
Péronne-Mons-en-Chaussée
Péronne-Bouvincourt
Roisel
Saint-Quentin-Roupy
Saint-Quentin
Cambrai
Cambrai-Niergnies
Denain

Monchy-Lagache
No 4 Sqn/Lysander
Besny-et-Loizy
Courbes
Couvron
Laon
Laon-Chambry
Ouise-Villers

BELGIUM

Villeneuve-les-Vertus
No 105 Sqn/Battle
Plivot
No 139 Sqn/Blenheim
Barry-au-Bac
No 1 Sqn/Hurricane
No 142 Sqn/Battle
Reims
No 73 Sqn/Hurricane
Amifontaine
No 14 Sqn/Battle

Condé-Vraux
No 114 Sqn/Blenheim
Écury-sur-coole
No 15 Sqn/Battle
Poix
No 59 Sqn/Blenheim
Mourmelon
No 88 Sqn/Battle
Béthenville
No 103 Sqn/Battle

Gamelin failed utterly to coordinate any counterattacks or revisions to Allied strategy when the German breakthrough at Sedan shattered that strategy and all its assumptions. After having dominated French defence policy for almost a decade, General Gamelin was relieved of duty on 18 May 1940 and replaced by his rival General Maxime Weygand.

General Joseph Vuillemin (1883–1963)

Joseph Vuillemin entered military service in 1904 and served as an enlisted man until 1909, when he became an officer cadet. He was commissioned an artillery lieutenant in 1910 and undertook flight training in 1913 and transferred to the French Aviation Service. During World War I, he earned a distinguished record as a bomber and reconnaissance pilot. Promoted to captain in 1916, he served as a reconnaissance squadron commander. He won fame as an aggressive pilot who used his two- and three-seater reconnaissance planes to attack German aircraft. He and his observer were credited with shooting down seven German aircraft. In 1918, Vuillemin was appointed as a bomber group commander in France's elite First Air Division. He ended the war as one of France's most highly decorated airmen, with a Légion d'honneur and the Croix de Guerre with ten palms.

In the 1920s, he won fame for leading pioneering long-distance flights across Africa. He was promoted to brigadier-general in 1933, and from 1935–36 he commanded l'Armée de l'Air's 1st Air Corps. In February 1938, Vuillemin was promoted to *Général D'armée Aérienne* and was appointed as Chief of Staff of the French Air Force. As Chief of Staff, Vuillemin supported the plan to purchase large numbers of aircraft from the United States, realizing the severe deficiencies of the French Air Force in numbers and quality of aircraft. Yet during his tenure as Air Force Chief of Staff, Vuillemin did little to deal with the enormous problem of the weak French infrastructure, logistics, and personnel systems.

Vuillemin insisted on expanding the pilot training program but took little action to ensure that the program succeeded. It was only after the start of the war in October 1939 that he responded to the appeals of the air force training commanders to create a specialist course for instructor pilots. Beyond establishing the air region command system, Vuillemin again did little to adapt command and control and French air doctrine to the requirements of modern warfare. The French Air Force went to war with virtually no reserve aircraft and without any standard system of ferrying replacement pilots and aircraft to front-line units.

Damage to a French military airfield during the first days of the May 1940 offensive. (AC)

France had no effective system for air defence warning. In short, Vuillemin had more than two years to fix an assortment of glaring management problems.

Following his superior Gamelin's guidance, Vuillemin argued strongly against any Allied bombing of Germany during the Phoney War in fear that the Luftwaffe might retaliate and attack French cities. Indeed, after Italy declared war on France and Britain on 11 June 1940, Vuillemin forbade the RAF from flying bomber missions against Italian cities, again fearing that the Italians would retaliate in kind. Throughout the 1940 campaign, Vuillemin argued repeatedly for more British air support, complaining that the British were not stripping Fighter Command aircraft to defend France, while at the same time holding back many of his own fighters in the French interior to defend the French cities. Vuillemin was heartily disliked by the British senior commanders. His chief subordinate, General d'Astier, who commanded the largest part of the French combat forces, complained that Vuillemin offered little guidance but 'vainglorious orders'. The view on Vuillemin from the perspective of the senior commanders was best expressed by the British attaché to Paris, who noted in May 1940, alluding to Vuillemin, that 'while some French senior officers had been very brave pilots in the last war, they were not sufficiently educated to command important formations now'. Much like the French Commander-in-Chief Gamelin, Vuillemin can be assessed as an exceptionally brave and competent officer in World War I who utterly failed as a senior commander in the next war.

General François d'Astier de La Vigerie (1886–1956)
François d'Astier came from a line of French nobility and professional soldiers. Commissioned as a lieutenant in the cavalry in 1911, he transferred to the French Air Service in 1915. He served as a fighter pilot in 1916, and as a squadron commander in 1917. He was credited as an ace with shooting down five German aircraft and awarded the Croix de Guerre. In the 1920s, d'Astier served in combat in Morocco, where he effectively supported French Army operations. In 1936, he was promoted to general and made commander of an air brigade.

General François d'Astier de La Vigerie, Commander of the Northern Air Zone (ZOAN) in 1940. (AC)

In September 1939, d'Astier was made commander of the Northern Air Zone (ZOAN), which contained most of the French Air Force's combat forces. D'Astier worked closely with the RAF air commander in France, Air Marshal Barratt, and ZOAN headquarters and British Air Forces France headquarters were collocated to ensure close cooperation. During the campaign in May 1940, d'Astier initiated several reforms, including removing fighters and reconnaissance squadrons from army command and placing them under ZOAN command. He even collected a force as a special assault group of modern bombers and fighters that he could employ in direct support of the army in the front lines. Yet he discovered in early June that the French Tenth Army commander was disinterested when offered this assault force to support a major attack.

In his post-war memoirs, *Le ciel n'était pas vide, 1940* (*The Sky Was Not Empty, 1940*) d'Astier blamed the French Army generals for their lack of understanding of modern joint warfare, and their disregard for employing the French Air Force in the ground battle. D'Astier recalled that during the campaign, every day he would contact the French Army commanders that he supported to ask for their air support requirements. Usually, he received no requests.

With the fall of France, d'Astier was transferred to North Africa as the air commander for Morocco. In July 1940, after the British had raided the French naval base at Mers-el-Kébir in North Africa, he refused a direct order from the Vichy government demanding that he bomb the British base at Gibraltar in retaliation. For this act, d'Astier was relieved of command, retired, and returned to France where he joined a resistance group set up by his brother Emmanuel d'Astier. In 1942, d'Astier escaped France and fled to England, where he joined General de Gaulle and served on de Gaulle's senior military committee. In 1943 and 1944, d'Astier worked with Supreme Allied Headquarters to plan for the invasion and liberation of France. D'Astier is regarded as one of the most capable of the French commanders of 1940, and his post-war account of the battle for France provides excellent insights into the dysfunction of the senior Allied commanders.

Air Chief Marshal Cyril Newall, Chief of the Air Staff (third left), accompanied by Air Commodore Londonderry and Air Vice Marshal Patrick Playfair (first left), on an RAF airfield in France in early 1940. (IWM)

Air Chief Marshal Cyril Newall (1886–1963)

Hailing from a family of military officers, Cyril Newall followed the family profession in 1905 to be commissioned an infantry lieutenant. As a young officer, he served in India, seeing combat on the north-west frontier. In 1911, Newall learned to fly and joined the RFC, serving as an instructor until August 1914, when he was made a flight commander and deployed to France. During World War I, as one of a small cadre of pre-war RFC officers, he moved up quickly. In 1916, he took command of an RFC bomber wing. In 1917, he was made a temporary brigadier-general. In early 1918, when General Trenchard set up an independent bomber force of large bombers to bomb the German homeland, Newall was appointed as Trenchard's second in command and spent the last year of the war involved in strategic bombing operations. In 1919, Newall was given a permanent rank of lieutenant-colonel in the new RAF. He held a series of RAF senior staff and command positions. By 1926, he was the director of operations and intelligence for the RAF Air Staff. In 1935, as an air marshal, Newall was placed in charge of the RAF supply and organization. Newall was seen by his RAF peers as a capable administrator, but it was also thought that he lacked the broad vision and leadership qualities to serve as chief of staff. Nonetheless, to the surprise of the RAF officer corps, in September 1937 he was appointed Chief of Staff of the RAF.

As RAF Chief of Supply and RAF Chief of Staff Newall was a central figure in British rearmament beginning in the mid-1930s. As a staunch disciple of Hugh Trenchard since World War I, Newall maintained that bombers were Britain's top priority. An array of new medium and light bombers – including the excellent Wellington medium bomber, the Blenheim light bomber, and the medium Whitley and Hampden bombers – made up the main force of Bomber Command at the outbreak of the war. Newall also ensured that heavy bomber programs were underway, which by 1941 would include the four-engine Stirling and Halifax heavy bombers, and in 1942, the Lancaster heavy bomber. While preferring Bomber Command, Newall had to bow to Britain's main defence policy, which since World War I had ensured that the British homeland was well-defended. So, against the view of many senior officers of the RAF, in 1937–38 Newall agreed to large expenditures for a much larger RAF force of Hurricanes and Spitfires.

It was largely through Newall's efforts that RAF rearmament was in full swing at the start of the war, and that aircraft production in Britain was soon to surpass that in Germany. As to how the RAF might be employed in a European war, Newall was a firm believer that strategic bombing of German industries could prove decisive, and he generally opposed using bombers in a ground battle, as being likely too expensive while being unlikely to lead to the decisive success that strategic bombing promised. In this, he was closely aligned with RAF top leadership, which had a deep aversion to using airpower tactically.

Newall's strategic bombing campaign against German industries was not only indecisive; it was basically a total washout, making some small, feeble strikes into Germany that caused minimal damage while leading not a single German aircraft to be brought back from the front lines to defend the Fatherland.

Due to the poor performance of the RAF in the Norway and France campaigns, Newall was fired, retired in October 1940, and was sent to serve as governor-general of New Zealand, a largely ceremonial position, until the end of the war.

Air Marshal Arthur Barratt (1891–1966)

Arthur Barratt joined the British Army as an artillery lieutenant in 1910. In 1914, he transferred to the RFC and became a squadron commander. Deployed to France in 1914, Barratt soon became commander of a reconnaissance/observation squadron. By the end of the war, he was a decorated wing commander. In 1924, Barratt attended the British Army Staff College at Camberley. Subsequently, he became a teacher at the RAF Staff College. Then in the 1930s, he served a tour as the commandant of the RAF Staff College.

In September 1939, Barratt, now an air marshal, was appointed as the principal RAF liaison officer to the French Air Force. As such, he would have routine disputes with French Air Force Chief of Staff Vuillemin concerning French support for British air units in France, an ongoing debate in which the French insisted on vetoing British proposals to use the AASF and RAF Bomber Command to attack targets in Germany. With two different RAF commands in France, both independent of each other, the AASF and the air component of the BEF, it was thought best to have a single commander over both RAF elements. Thus, in January 1940, Barratt took over command of the BAFF (British Air Forces France) and set up his headquarters in Chauny, alongside the headquarters of the French Air Force's Northern Operational Zone (ZOAN), which was commanded by General François d'Astier de La Vigerie. Barratt and d'Astier formed a good working relationship that ensured that the two air forces would share air defence responsibilities and that British and French fighter units would cooperate to escort and support each other's bomber and reconnaissance missions.

Barratt was in a difficult position as commander, largely due to questions about his command authority and the level of support that he might get from the RAF Air Staff. Although he had some authority to employ the AASF on tactical missions, that force basically belonged to Bomber Command, headquartered in Britain, who would need to be consulted before Barratt issued mission orders. As to whether bombers could be used tactically, RAF Bomber Command promised that the BEF would be supported by Bomber Command if conditions required it. But this left a lot of questions unanswered. From his arrival as the RAF representative to the French in September 1939, Barratt had to deal with a host of logistics and support issues as the French Air Force, burdened with its own logistics problems, had little to spare in support of the RAF. During late 1939 and early 1940, the RAF, which was used to flying out of permanent bases in Britain, had to establish itself at several primitive French airfields that usually lacked maintenance facilities, anti-aircraft protection, or effective communications. However, upon taking command of the BAFF, Barratt initiated some major changes by setting up RAF liaison teams with vehicles and radios that could operate with the BEF corps and divisions. Just like the German air liaison officers (FLIVOs), the RAF teams provided Barratt with a constant flow of information on the ground and air situation, enabling Barratt to make decisions to employ his available bombers and fighters. This liaison system and good communications made it possible for the RAF to generate

Air Chief Arthur Barratt, Commander of the British Air Forces France (BAFF), standing next to his personal Hurricane that he used to visit his air units. (IWM)

more missions and sorties than its counterparts in the French Air Force, who had a much less effective army/air force liaison. After the 1940 campaign, Barratt served in major training positions and ended the war as RAF Inspector General. But he was not again offered a combat command.

Air Marshal Patrick Playfair (1889–1974)

Patrick Playfair was commissioned a lieutenant in the Royal Artillery in 1910. In 1912, he underwent pilot training and transferred to the RFC. During World War I, he rose through the ranks, serving first as a squadron, and then a wing commander. He was accepted into the RAF at the rank of lieutenant-colonel after the war. In the 1920s, Playfair served as air commander in Palestine and in India. Returning to the United Kingdom in 1932, Playfair was assigned to Bomber Command. Then, in 1938, he took command of Bomber Command's No. 1 Group.

Within Bomber Command, Playfair was known to be something of a gadfly. During the 1930s, he was denied promotion for his criticism of Bomber Command's commander and staff for being far too distant from the actual units in terms of the operational requirements for the bomber wings and groups, criticism that proved quite accurate.

In September 1939, Playfair was given command of the AASF, which was largely built out of squadrons from No. 1 Group that he had commanded. Playfair was in an awkward position in serving both Air Marshal Barratt and the BAFF while serving as part of Bomber Command at the same time, which did not offer much guidance as to how his light Battle bombers might be best employed. In his desire to fully support the BEF, Playfair initiated his own training program for the Battle squadrons, practising low-level attacks against front-line targets, which would likely be necessary when the Germans invaded the Low Countries like the Allies anticipated. Playfair discussed the possibilities of adapting the Battle bomber as an assault plane, which could best be accomplished by removing the large fuel tank and the fuselage along with the third Battle crew member, the navigator, and replacing that weight with extra armour, self-sealing fuel tanks, and additional armament. If that had been done, it would have made the Battle bomber into an at least adequate bomber plane, but Bomber Command still viewed the Battles and the AASF as a strategic force and discouraged any adaptation of the force into a tactical one.

Playfair was a highly practical and pragmatic commander whose main problem in employing his AASF was the little-to-no guidance that he received from Bomber Command.

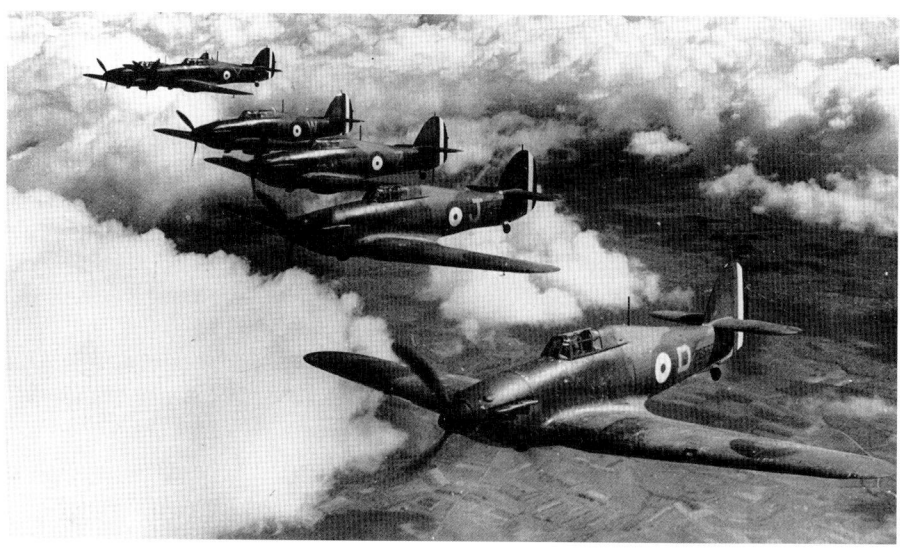

The flight of a squadron of Hawker Hurricanes demonstrating the tight echelon formations from Fighter Command's tactical manual. (AC)

ORDERS OF BATTLE – ALLIED FORCES
FRENCH ARMY – GÉNÉRAL D'ARMÉE MAURICE GAMELIN

Théâtre d'opérations du nord-est – général d'armée alphonse-joseph georges
Réserves du Grand Quartier Général (GQG)
1ère Division Cuirassée
2e Division Cuirassée
3e Division Cuirassée
21e Corps d'Armée
23e Corps d'Armée
Reserve Divisions
10e DI
14e DI
23e DI
28e DI
29e DI
36e DI
43e DI
3e DIM
1ère DINA
7e DINA
5e DIC
7e DIC
2e DIP
GROUPE D'ARMÉES 1 – GÉNÉRAL D'ARMÉE GASTON H. T. BILLOTTE
1ère Armée – Général Jean Georges Blanchard
2e Division Légère Mécanique
3e Division Légère Mécanique
3e Corps d'Armée
1ère Division d'Infanterie Motorisée
2e Division d'Infanterie Nord Afrique
4e Corps d'Armée
15e Division d'Infanterie Motorisée
1ère Division d'Infanterie Marocaine
5e Corps d'Armée
12e Division d'Infanterie Motorisée
5e Division d'Infanterie Nord-Africaine
101ère Division d'Infanterie de Forteresse
Réserve de l'Armée
32e Division d'Infanterie
2e Armée – Général d'Armée Charles Huntziger
2e Division Légère de Cavalerie
5e Division Légère de Cavalerie
1ère Brigade de Chasseurs
Secteur Fortifié de Montmédy
10e Corps d'Armée
55e Division d'Infanterie
3e Division d'Infanterie Nord-Africaine

18e Corps d'Armée
41e Division d'Infanterie
1ère Division d'Infanterie Coloniale
3e Division d'Infanterie Coloniale
Réserve de l'Armée
71e Division d'Infanterie
7e Armée – Général d'Armée Henri Giraud
21e Division d'Infanterie
60e Division d'Infanterie
68e Division d'Infanterie
16e Corps d'Armée
1ère DLM Division Légère Mécanique
25e Division d'Infanterie Motorisée
9e Division d'Infanterie Motorisée
9e Armée – Général d'Armée André Georges Corap
1ère Division Légère de Cavalerie
4e Division Légère de Cavalerie
3e Spahi Brigade
2e Corps d'Armée
5e Division d'Infanterie Motorisée
11e Corps d'Armée
18e Division d'Infanterie
22e Division d'Infanterie
41e Corps d'Armée de Forteresse
61e Division d'Infanterie
102e Division d'Infanterie de Forteresse
Réserve de l'Armée
4e Division d'Infanterie Nord Africaine
53e Division d'Infanterie

L'ARMÉE DE L'AIR
Forces Aériennes de Cooperation du Front Nord-Est
Zone d'Operations Aériennes Nord – Général François d'Astier de La Vigerie
(NOTE: Numbers represent serviceable aircraft strength on 10 May 1940)
Groupement de Chasse 23

GC II/2	22 M.S.406s
GC III/2	28 M.S.406s
GC I/525 H-75s	
ECMH 1/16	10 Potez 631s

Tactical Reconnaissance

GR II/22	Potez 63-11s (Second Army)
GR II/52	Potez 637/63-11s (Ninth Army)

Bombers
1ère Division Aérienne – Général Escudier

GR I/52	10 Potez 637s
GR II/33	6 Bloch MB.174s

No. 6 Groupement de Bombardement de Jour
GB I/12   7 LeO 451s
GB II/12   7 LeO 451s
No. 9 Groupement de Bombardement de Jour
GB I/34   8 Amiot 143s
GB II/34   9 Amiot 143s
Groupement de Bombardement d'Assaut
No. 18 Groupement de Bombardement
GBA I/54   13 Breguet 693s
GBA II/54   12 Breguet 693s

Strategic Reconnaissance
GR II/33   13 Potez 637/63-11s and 6
Bloch MB.174s
Aéronautique Navale
AC 1 12 Potez 63
AC2 12 Potez 63
AB 1 12 LN 401s
AB 4 12 LN 411s
F 1A Flotilla du Béarn
AB 2 12 LN 401
AB 3 12 Vought V 156

BRITISH FORCES

British Expeditionary Force (BEF) – General Lord Gort
I Corps
1st Division
2nd Division
48th (South Midland) Division
II Corps
3rd Division
4th Division
50th Division
III Corps
42nd (East Lancashire) Division
44th (Home Counties) Division
Line of Communication Troops
12th (Eastern) Division
23rd (Northumbrian) Division
46th (North Midland and West Riding) Division
General Headquarters (GHQ) Forces
5th Division (BEF Reserve)
1st Tank Brigade
1st and 2nd Armoured Reconnaissance Brigades
1st and 2nd Regiments, Royal Horse Artillery
Four medium field artillery regiments
Eight medium, three heavy, and three super-heavy
artillery regiments
1st, 2nd, and 4th AA Brigades
(Note: 51st (Highland) Division attached to French 3e
Armée behind the Maginot Line)

ROYAL AIR FORCE
**British Air Forces in France (BAFF) – Air
Marshal Barratt**
**Advanced Air Striking Force – Air Vice
Marshal Playfair**
Fighters: 67 (Fighter) Wing
1 Squadron   Hurricanes Is
73 Squadron   Hurricane Is
501 Squadron Hurricane Is

Bombers
71 (Bomber) Wing
105 Squadron   Battle Is
114 Squadron   Blenheim IVs
139 Squadron   Blenheim IVs
150 Squadron   Battle Is
75 (Bomber) Wing
88 Squadron   Battle Is
103 Squadron   Battle Is
218 Squadron   Battle Is
76 (Bomber) Wing
12 Squadron   Battle Is
142 Squadron   Battle Is
226 Squadron   Battle Is

Air Component BEF – Air Vice Marshal Blount
50 Wing Army Cooperation
4 Squadron ACU Lysanders
13 Squadron ACU Lysanders
16 Squadron ACU Lysanders
51 Wing Army Cooperation
2 Squadron ACU Lysanders
26 Squadron ACU Lysanders
52 Wing Bombers
53 Squadron Blenheims
59 Squadron Blenheims
70 Wing Bombers
18 Squadron Blenheims
57 Squadron Blenheims
14 Group
61 Wing
607 Squadron Hurricanes
615 Squadron Hurricanes
60 Wing
85 Squadron Hurricanes
87 Squadron Hurricanes
63 Wing
3 Squadron Hurricanes
79 Squadron Hurricanes

CAMPAIGN OBJECTIVES
Opposing strategies 1939–40

The rise of Nazi power in the 1930s pushed the French and British governments to discuss joint military action and the two powers agreed that if war came the two nations would form a military alliance and Britain would send an army and air units to France to operate alongside the French forces. The BEF would serve under a French army group and the RAF contingent would operate closely with the French Air Force. French military Commander-in-Chief General Maurice Gamelin would serve as the military supreme commander of the Allied forces in France and would lead the military council that determined Allied strategy. France, with its 90-division army, would be the senior partner of the alliance in terms of any land and air battles on the continent.

When Germany started the war by invading Poland, Britain responded by sending the BEF and a strong air contingent to France, beginning in September 1939. The initial BEF was eight divisions but was expected to grow to 14 divisions. The Allied Powers correctly assumed that the Germans would turn their attention west after Poland was defeated and developed plans accordingly. Realizing Germany's strong military position, the Allied strategy was highly defensive. This defensive mindset was based on the assumption that while the Allies were too weak to go on the offensive, France's army could not be defeated if it held strong defensive positions. France had its border with Germany covered by the massive forts of the Maginot Line. The northern border was not covered by such powerful forts but there were rivers and canals that, if well-defended, were ideal barriers against any German advance.

In the early months of the war, the Allies expected that Germany's most likely move would be an invasion of the neutral Low Countries. Thus, Allied planning focused on deploying the elite armoured and mechanized forces of the French Army along with the fully motorized BEF, a force of 30 divisions, as an army group ready to immediately deploy into Belgium and the Netherlands if Germany invaded. There, the British and French forces would join with the Belgian and Dutch armies and set up a strong defence behind river and canal lines in central Belgium and the southern Netherlands that made excellent anti-tank barriers. The strategy was to halt, but not defeat, any German advance. This plan appealed to the French as they had

A French rail junction destroyed by Luftwaffe bombers during preparations for *Fall Rot*. The Luftwaffe prepared for the final offensive beginning 5 June by major attacks on rail junctions throughout northern and central France to disrupt any French troop movements. (Alamy)

An Allied column under attack by German medium bombers in May 1940. (AC)

experienced the devastation of much of northern France in the last war, and in this war they preferred to see the fighting done on other nations' territory.

In February, General Gamelin approved the Allied strategic plan to move the First Army Group (French 1st, 7th, 9th Armies and the BEF) into Belgium and the Netherlands if the Germans invaded those countries. It was called the Dyle Plan as the Allied First Army Group would move and then defend the line behind the Dyle River in Belgium. A core assumption of the British and French governments and armies was that the French army, if placed behind fortifications or strong defensive positions, could not be defeated by the Germans.

The German war plans indeed anticipated that Germany would go on the offence and attack and overrun the Low Countries in a European war. While having small and capable armies and air forces, neither Belgium nor the Netherlands could stand for long against German military superiority. The Germans also correctly assumed that the French and British would advance into the Low Countries to engage the German forces. The German plan was largely a repeat of the World War I Schlieffen Plan, but this time Panzer, motorized, and airborne forces, along with strong air support, would allow for a much speedier timetable. Army Group B in the north would contain most of Germany's Panzer divisions and would be the main force for the offensive. Army Group A in the centre would play a supporting role and Army Group C, a collection of infantry divisions, would simply hold the area of the Maginot Line where it faced an equal number of French divisions. The German *Fall Gelb* (Case Yellow) plan for the attack in the west was approved by Hitler in October 1939, and Hitler demanded that the attack should begin as soon as possible. But the plan required good weather, and the winter of 1939–40 was one of the coldest in many years; thus the attack was postponed again and again through the winter. However, spring weather would finally allow the plan to proceed.

The plan itself, which came from the Army General Staff, was doubted by many among the army leadership, most notably General Erich von Manstein, Chief of Staff of Army Group A. Army Group A's Commander Generaloberst Gerd von Rundstedt disliked the plan as it provided no real decisive result other than gaining ground and improving Germany's strategic position. The winter of 1939–40, Von Manstein developed a different concept, which was to shift most of the Panzer and motorized forces to Army Group A, at the centre of the front. The main thrust of the German offensive would advance through Luxembourg, Belgium, and northern France, through the Ardennes region, to cross the Meuse at Sedan near the French border and then, with a powerful armoured and motorized force, drive quickly through the Allied centre to the English Channel at Abbeville, thus cutting off the Allied Northern Army Group, which contained the best divisions of the French Army as well as the whole of the BEF.

Cut off from their logistics and surrounded, with Army Group A to the south and Army Group B to the north, not only would the Low Countries fall to the German onslaught, but the best of the Allied ground forces could be trapped and destroyed, leaving the Germans in position to drive south and overrun France. There was considerable interest in Von Manstein's concept, which Von Rundstedt wholeheartedly supported, but the Army High Command remained fixed on the original plan.

However, an accident forced the German High Command to rethink its Western Front offensive, when a small liaison plane carrying a staff of officers from Luftflotte 2 strayed into Belgian airspace in bad weather and crash-landed in Belgian territory. Before the Luftwaffe staff officer could destroy the plan, he and the aircraft were surrounded and captured by Belgian soldiers. The outlines of the plan were leaked to the French and British, which readily confirmed to them what they had already assumed: that the Germans' next major move would be an invasion of the Low Countries.

Now that the German Army's campaign plan was revealed to the Allies, General Hellmuth Felmy, whose liaison aircraft had gone down in Belgium, was relieved of command and replaced by General der Flieger Albert Kesselring. The events of January provided an opportunity for Von Manstein to brief Hitler and present his concept of operations. He pushed the General Staff to formally review his ideas, which were adopted by the High Command in March 1940, with the bulk of Germany's elite Panzer and motorized divisions to be shifted to Army Group A and concentrated into a mobile army under the command of General der Kavallerie Ewald von Kleist. Panzergruppe Kleist would be the armoured spearhead to punch through at Sedan, then straight across northern France.

The Luftwaffe's plans were changed accordingly. The Air Fleet commanders, General der Flieger Kesselring in the north and General der Flieger Hugo Sperrle commanding Luftflotte 3 in the centre, undertook intensive planning, considering how the German Army could use the help of Luftwaffe reconnaissance to break through the Allied centre.

The new German concept of operations counted on the Allies reacting quickly to the German invasion of the Low Countries and falling into a trap. France had built a deep line of massive forts and defences along the Maginot Line. But this fortress line ended south of Sedan, and the French-Belgian border had no such prepared fortifications. Shortly before the war, a secondary defensive line of bunkers was begun along the vulnerable section of border facing the Ardennes. However, by May 1940, not all the bunkers had been completed, and the French soldiers of the Second Army were Class B infantry divisions comprised reservists over 30, who had little military training since their conscript service had been more than a decade before. Moreover, there were very few regular officers assigned to them, so that they were commanded mostly by reserve officers with relatively little serious training. The French plans for defence of this sector included vast minefields to be laid and additional fortifications to be built. The French Second Army spent the winter mainly trying to stay warm. Despite being one of the most effective tank weapons ever to appear, few mines were laid. Also, unlike the German Army, the French Army conducted little in the way of operational training.

The Ardennes, on the east side of the Meuse in Luxembourg in western Belgium, featured terrain of steep, heavily forested hills, plateaux, and deep valleys. It was not good country for armour, but it was made more passable in the 1920s and 1930s when the Belgian government improved the road network through the Ardennes, hoping to attract tourists to the scenic area. The French General Staff had held wargames in the 1930s in which a German advance through the Ardennes was posed, but the French concluded that German motorized forces could be delayed by roadblocks and screening forces, and it might take up to ten days to traverse the Ardennes. Thus, if the Germans attacked, the French Army would have time to send forces to the Sedan sector and defeat any German attack. For the German plan to succeed, they needed to reach the Meuse in three days and be ready to cross the river in overwhelming force by the fourth day if *Fall Gelb* was to succeed.

A Farman NC.222, a product of the French Air Force's BCR Aircraft Programme of the early 1930s. It was slow and underpowered. However, it still constituted a part of the French bomber arm and was still in use in the 1940 campaign. (Alamy)

THE CAMPAIGN

The air battle for the West

Opening the battle

The German Army and air doctrine emphasized concentration of forces and using them in a massive blow at the decisive point. From 10 to 13 May 1940, the decisive point of the campaign for the French and British forces was the German offensive in the Low Countries. For the first four days of the campaign, the BEF and most of the French Army's mechanized and motorized divisions were thrown into Belgium and the Netherlands. Army Group B invaded the Low Countries early on 10 May with major paratroop drops to seize key airfields deep in the Netherlands at the same moment that Panzer and infantry divisions crossed the Belgian and Dutch borders. The paratroop landings by the 7th Fallschirmjäger Division employed nearly the whole of the Luftwaffe's 500 transport planes. Rapid and fierce resistance by local Dutch forces contained the landings and destroyed many of the German transport aircraft by artillery and air attacks by the Dutch Air Force. Other transports were forced to land on boggy ground and were immobilized. Half of the Luftwaffe's transports were destroyed or badly damaged on 10 May. The seizure of the bridges at Rotterdam by German paratroops, however, did succeed, and despite Dutch counterattacks managed to hold on until Panzer units reached them on 13 May. By taking the bridges at Rotterdam, the Germans had pierced the final Dutch defence line for the southern Netherlands.

In western Belgium, the army's XVI Motorized Corps had seized three key bridges across the Albert Canal at Maastricht which were essential for Army Group B's advance into Belgium. The Luftwaffe's prowess in air operations was demonstrated when the Allies tried to destroy these bridges. On 11 May, the Belgian Air Force sent nine of its Battle bombers to destroy the bridges. The attack failed and six Battles were shot down by fighters and flak. The Germans established a strong flak defence around the bridges, and when the AASF attacked with five Battles escorted by eight Hurricanes on 12 May, five of the Hurricanes were shot down and three badly damaged while all the Battles were lost, four from flak and one from a Bf 109. In total 24 Bomber Command Blenheim bombers attacked, ten were shot down,

and four were damaged beyond repair. A French attack by 18 new Breguet 693 bombers saw ten shot down by German flak. The bridges remained unharmed.

While Luftflotte 2 was heavily engaged in the Low Countries, Luftflotte 3 carried out a series of attacks on French airfields. Some squadrons were shattered but damage was moderate. Still, it was a blow to the French Air Force, which had no reserves of aircraft to replace losses. In the meantime, the Allied 1st Army Group consisting of the BEF and the French First, Seventh, and Ninth Armies, the best motorized and armoured forces of the Allied armies, advanced per the Dyle Plan into Belgium and the southern Netherlands and set up a strong defensive line to stop Army Group B's advance – just as the Germans had hoped.

Meanwhile, German Army Group A pushed quickly through the Ardennes in three days, brushing aside the light cavalry and mechanized scout units in that sector. By 12 May, it emerged out of the Ardennes on a 25-mile front overlooking Sedan and the Meuse River.

The German offensive in the centre was spearheaded by Panzergruppe von Kleist, commanded by General der Kavallerie Ewald von Kleist. Panzergruppe von Kleist consisted of five Panzer divisions and three motorized infantry divisions, organized into two corps. Generalleutnant Georg-Hans Reinhardt's XLIst Armeekorps (motorized) (which would cross the Meuse to the north-west of Sedan) and General Heinz Guderian's XIX Panzerkorps, consisting of the 1st, 2nd, and 10th Panzer Divisions with the attached Infanterie Regiment Grossdeutschland, a motorized formation. It was Guderian's XIX Panzerkorps that would spearhead the main attack on Sudan. The German Army had concentrated half of the army's available tanks in Von Kleist's army, having swallowed the German Army's concept that it was 'better to strike with your fist than to feel with your fingers'.

The French defensive line at Sedan was a naturally strong position. At this point, the Meuse River was 200ft wide and deep, a natural anti-tank barrier. On the west bank of the Meuse in this sector, the riverline was overlooked by a long ridgeline – the 1,000ft-high Marfée Heights, steep and heavily wooded. The Sedan sector lay north of the Maginot Line and before the war 42 concrete blockhouses and pillboxes defended this sector. It seemed improbable that the Germans would attack this sector, so it was guarded mainly by the French 55th Infantry Division, a Class B French reserve division, meaning that its soldiers were reservists over 30 years of age. The officers were nearly all reservists as well, with very

A Dewoitine D.520 fighter plane, France's best fighter plane in 1940. Fast and highly manoeuvrable, armed with 120mm cannon and four 7.5mm machine guns, the D.520 could match the performance of the Luftwaffe's Bf 109 fighters. The D.520 only arrived to equip French fighter units in May 1940. (AC)

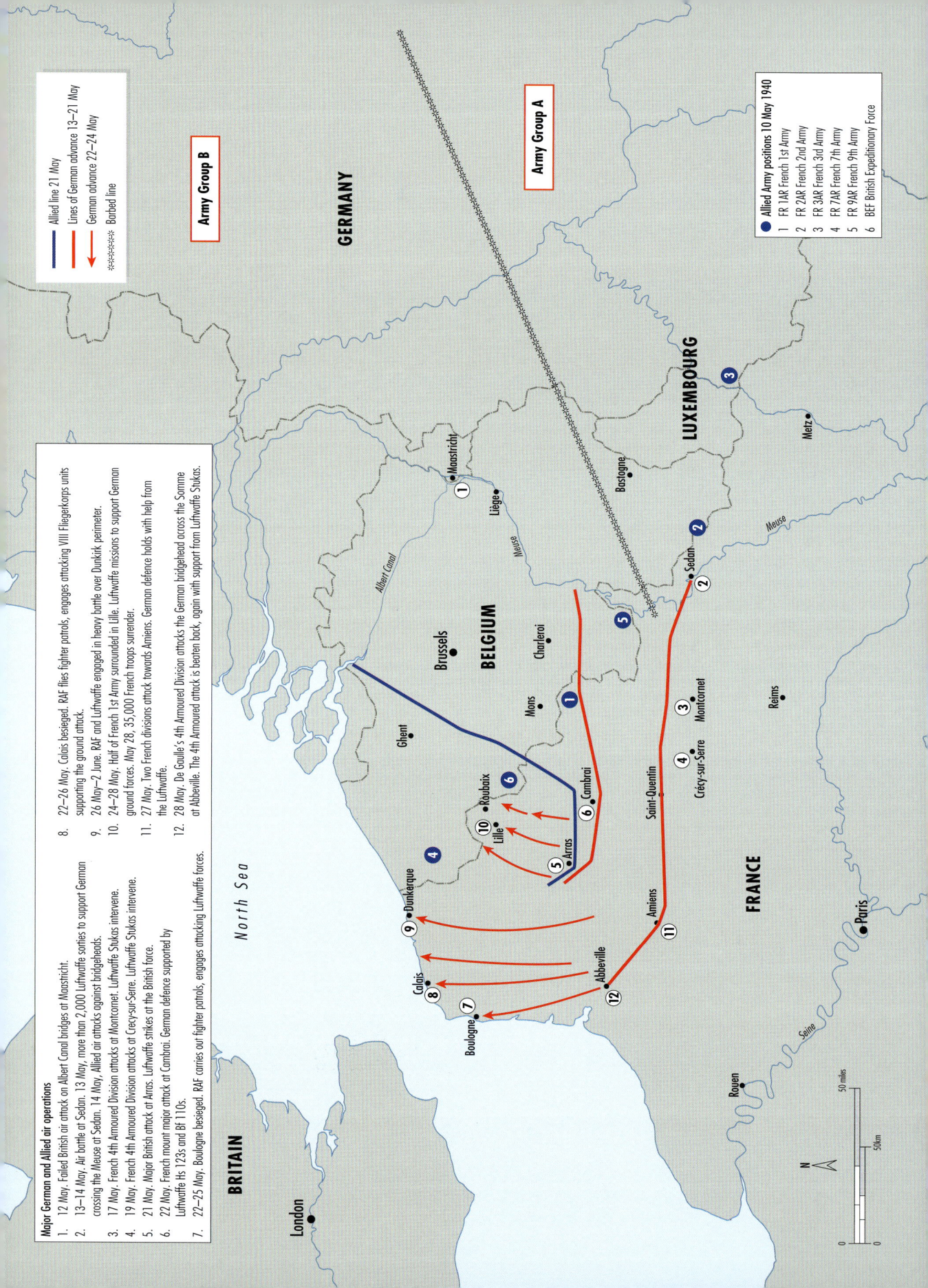

Major German and Allied air operations

1. 12 May. Foiled British air attack on Albert Canal bridges at Maastricht.
2. 13–14 May. Air battle at Sedan. 13 May, more than 2,000 Luftwaffe sorties to support German crossing the Meuse at Sedan. 14 May, Allied air attacks against bridgeheads.
3. 17 May, French 4th Armoured Division attacks at Montcornet. Luftwaffe Stukas intervene.
4. 19 May, French 4th Armoured Division attacks at Crecy-sur-Serre. Luftwaffe Stukas intervene.
5. 21 May, Major British attack at Arras. Luftwaffe strikes at the British force.
6. 22 May, French mount major attack at Cambrai. German defence supported by Luftwaffe Hs 123s and Bf 110s.
7. 22–25 May. Boulogne besieged. RAF carries out fighter patrols, engages attacking Luftwaffe forces.
8. 22–26 May. Calais besieged. RAF flies fighter patrols, engages attacking VIII Fliegerkops units supporting the ground attack.
9. 26 May–2 June. RAF and Luftwaffe engaged in heavy battle over Dunkirk perimeter.
10. 24–28 May. Half of French 1st Army surrounded in Lille. Luftwaffe missions to support German ground forces. May 28, 35,000 French troops surrender.
11. 27 May. Two French divisions attack towards Amiens. German defence holds with help from the Luftwaffe.
12. 28 May. De Gaulle's 4th Armoured Division attacks the German bridgehead across the Somme at Abbeville. The 4th Armoured attack is beaten back, again with support from Luftwaffe Stukas.

Allied Army positions 10 May 1940

● 1 FR 1AR French 1st Army
2 FR 2AR French 2nd Army
3 FR 3AR French 3rd Army
4 FR 7AR French 7th Army
5 FR 9AR French 9th Army
6 BEF British Expeditionary Force

— Allied line 21 May
— Lines of German advance 13–21 May
→ German advance 22–24 May
╬╬╬╬╬╬ Barbed line

Army Group B

Army Group A

GERMANY

LUXEMBOURG

BELGIUM

FRANCE

BRITAIN

North Sea

London
Maastricht
Liège
Bastogne
Metz
Sedan
Brussels
Charleroi
Mons
Ghent
Reims
Montcornet
Crecy-sur-Serre
Cambrai
Saint-Quentin
Roubaix
Lille
Arras
Dunkerque
Amiens
Abbeville
Calais
Boulogne
Paris
Rouen

Albert Canal
Meuse
Meuse
Seine

N

50 miles
50km

OPPOSITE OPENING MOVES, 10–14 MAY

few regular officers. As the Germans approached the Meuse another Class B reserve division, the 71st Infantry Division, was ordered to the Sedan sector, but only some elements had arrived when the battle began.

At the outbreak of the war, the French Army decided to add a further 61 concrete bunkers to the Sedan defence sector. These additional blockhouses included both large, reinforced-concrete bunkers holding ten to 12 soldiers armed with anti-tank guns, and small concrete pillboxes armed with a machine gun and a two-man crew. This would have made for a strong defence had it not been for France's lack of urgency in fortifying this sector. General Guderian was initially concerned about mounting a frontal assault against such fortifications and Generaloberst von Rundstedt, Army Group A Commander, requested extensive aerial reconnaissance from the Luftwaffe. Upon close examination of aerial photographs, it was revealed that many of the bunkers were still under construction, and other bunkers lacked basic security such as steel doors to their rear or steel shutters to protect the gunports from direct fire. This meant there were several weak spots on the first French defensive line along the river, so that if German infantry could cross the river, they could work their way behind the strongpoints and attack them from their poorly protected rear.

At Sedan, the French forward defence line consisted of concrete bunkers and fortifications right behind the Meuse and was manned by the regular army troops of the 147th Fortress Regiment. At Sedan, the main defence line was about a mile behind and consisted of a belt of more bunkers and field fortifications and artillery positions manned by the French 55th Infantry Division.

The French defence of the Meuse River at Sedan relied on artillery. In the Sedan sector, the 55th Division and corps artilley had 174 artillery pieces, not counting the anti-tank guns in the bunkers along the river. The heavy guns of the French 10th and 41st Army Corps flanking the sector could also be brought against parts of the Sedan sector. Guderian's XIXth Panzerkorps had only 141 motorized artillery pieces. Moreover, German Army artillery had only limited ammunition stocks that had advanced with the forward units, and the German attackers would be heavily outgunned by the defenders. In the French Army wargames of the 1930s, a scenario in which the Germans advanced through the Ardennes had been considered,

XIX Panzerkorps' Panzer II tanks and support vehicles, massing for an advance after crossing the Meuse on 14 May 1940. (AC)

but in this scenario, as the Allied High Command assumed, any German attackers would be forced to pause upon reaching the Meuse and bring up artillery, giving the French Army plenty of time to reinforce the sector.

However, General der Kavallerie von Kleist and Army Group A had planned very carefully for the Sedan attack. The movement through the 70 miles of the Ardennes was to take no more than three days so the XIXth Panzerkorps could arrive on 12 May and cross the river the next day. Crossing points and bridge sites had been allocated to each of the three divisions making the assult.

Luftwaffe signal troops setting up communications lines on a recently captured airfield in May 1940. The Luftwaffe's mobile support units could put a captured airfield into full operation within a day. (AC)

The movement plan ensured that engineers and bridge columns would travel up front close to the tanks. Plenty of flak would be available to protect the German force and to provide additional direct fire support. Instead of artillery, the XIXth Panzerkorps would rely on the Luftwaffe as flying artillery.

Panzergruppe von Kleist's forces arrived through the hills overlooking Sedan at noon on 12 May, having brushed aside the thin screen of the French 5th Cavalry Division after an impressive advance of 70 miles in two and a half days. Yet the French High Command was not overly concerned. The French commanders estimated that they had four to six days to reinforce the Sedan area while the Germans would have to bring up a large amount of artillery and ammunition to support any river crossing. Given a few days, the French could mass local reserves and tank units and more artillery to make an impregnable defence. They never reckoned that the Germans would attack the next day using aircraft as a substitute for artillery.

In early May, Guderian and Generalleutnant Bruno Loerzer, commander of II Fliegerkorps, had developed a detailed plan for air/ground cooperation. The French defences at Sedan were divided into sectors and all the blockhouses, strongpoints, and known artillery positions were given target numbers. The Luftwaffe would begin a heavy preparatory air bombardment for six hours before the infantry of the Panzer divisions would cross the Meuse by assault boats at 1500hrs. The Stukas would target the French forward defence line, each Stuka given specific targets. The Luftwaffe light and medium bombers would keep the main defence line and artillery positions under constant bombardment, attacking in group strength. As each Stuka or bomber group finished its bombing, the next group would arrive to attack. Stukas and the escort fighters would fly three or four sorties to Sedan that day. The bomber groups would fly a mission and return to their bases in Germany. They would rearm and refuel for a second sortie. The continous bombing would keep the French artillerymen in their shelters and prevent them from firing. At 1500hrs, as the crossing began, the Stukas would shift their bombing from the forward defence line to the main defence line as the infantry began the river crossing under supporting fire from the Panzer division's tanks, artillery, and attached flak guns firing at the bunkers from close range.

On 12 May, almost all of Hugo Sperrle's Luftflotte 3 was ordered to support the river crossing at Sedan. Generalmajor Wolfram von Richthofen's VIII Fliegerkorps, then engaged in support of Army Group B's advance through Belgium in the north, was transferred to Luftflotte 3 and told to support the attack at Sedan the next day. On such short notice, Von Richthofen could not redirect all his units from the continuing battle. He did, however, ensure that part of his bombers and fighters, most noticeably the Sturzkampfgeschwader 77, equipped with the Ju 87B aircraft, would be ready for the attack. At the last minute, General der Kavallerie von Kleist requested that instead of a continuous bombardment of the French positions, Sperrle was to carry out a single, massive strike to overwhelm the French. Sperrle agreed and initiated orders, but it was simply too late for the plans to change, so the air corps commanders stuck with the original plan: to bombard the French positions starting at 0800hrs on 13 May and to attack for eight hours.

With the confusion of organizing the Luftwaffe attack and moving Guderian's three Panzer divisions down to the Meuse on the morning of the 13th, the German air attack was delayed for an hour and a half, starting at 0930hrs. Guderian had been allocated the Luftwaffe's Flak Regiment 102 to support his attacks and the 1st, 2nd, and 10th Panzer Divisions had moved to the crossing sectors by 1200hrs and soon had their tank guns and flak guns targeting the French bunkers at each crossing point.

Soon after the air attack began, some of the French 55th Division units posted in the forward defence line began to retreat, stunned by the bombing. While the 10th Panzer and 2nd Panzer Divisions on the flanks took fire from French heavy artillery outside the Sedan sector, the 1st Panzer Division in the centre received little fire from the French artillery – thanks to the Luftwaffe's continuous bombing of the main defence line and French artillery positions. At 1500hrs, when the assault crossing began, the infantry of the 1st Panzer Division and attached Infanterie Regiment Grossdeutschland made rapid progress through the French forward defence. The 10th Panzer Division made slower progress but got enough infantry across the Meuse to start clearing the French first defence line. The 2nd Panzer Division had the toughest time and could not cross the Meuse in the face of fierce French resistance. But the progress of the 1st Panzer Division threatened the flanks of the French facing the 10th and 2nd Panzer Division crossing sites, and by late afternoon they were making progress. By early evening, the 1st Panzer Division troops were through the main line of defence. At 1830hrs, a false report that German tanks were advancing nearby reached the artillery units behind the main defence line. Some units panicked and abandoned their guns, and fled to the rear (the Germans would capture 28 abandoned guns the next day). This set off a chain reaction where most of the 55th Division and troops just arrived from the 71st Division abandoned the lines and fled several miles to the rear. The German engineers began building bridges for the tanks and set up ferry pontoons to bring reconnaissance vehicles, anti-tank units, and flak guns across the Meuse. The bridge in the 1st Panzer sector was completed at midnight and the one in the 10th Panzer sector at 0600hrs the next morning. The bridge in the 2nd Panzer Division's sector was only started the morning of the 14th. By 2200hrs on the 13th, German infantry had advanced 4 miles from the Meuse and found weak resistance in front of them. All night, the Germans put more troops across the Meuse, and early on

A French column caught on the road by the Luftwaffe in May 1940. A major part of Luftwaffe operations in 1940 was the disruption of Allied troop movements by air attack. (AC)

Key:

- ~~~~~ French forward defence line
- ——— French main defence line
- ⟶ German ground forces
- ● French artillery
- ★ River crossings
- 🚫 Axis bombing

EVENTS

1 12 May, midday. XIX Panzerkorps arrives north of Sedan. Units of the French 5th Cavalry Division retreat. The French Army evacuates Sedan and the north side of the Meuse and blows up all the bridges. French commanders estimate that the Germans will require four to six days to bring up artillery and ammunition sufficient to support a river crossing. This gives the French Army plenty of time to bring up strong reinforcements.

2 13 May, 0500–1200hrs. Three Panzer divisions and support troops advance to the Meuse crossing points.

3 1100hrs. Some of the 55th Division infantry on the forward defence line begin retreating, unnerved by the German air bombardment.

4 1300hrs. The assaulting Panzer divisions bring up tanks, flak guns and some artillery to pour direct fire into French forward defence bunkers at the crossing points.

5 1500hrs. The crossings begin at all sectors. The 1st Panzer Division makes two successful crossings, the 2nd Panzer Division fails to get troops across. 10th Panzer gets some infantry across and begins clearing the French forward defences.

6 1600hrs. The 1st Infantry Regiment of the 1st Panzer Division, and the Infanterie Regiment Grossdeutschland (mot.), make rapid progress breaking through the French forward defence line. Success in the central sector helps the 2nd and 10th Panzer Divisions move more infantry across as the French bunker line can now be attacked from the flanks and rear.

7 1800hrs. German engineers build pontoon bridges in the 1st and 10th Division sectors and set up pontoon ferries taking armoured cars, anti-tank guns and flak guns across the Meuse to fortify the bridgehead. A bridge in the 1st Division sector is completed by 2400hrs. The bridge in the 10th Panzer Division sector near Wadelincourt is completed by 0700hrs on 14 May. The bridge in the 2nd Panzer Division sector by Donchery is begun 14 May.

8 1830hrs. A false report that German tanks are across the Meuse and about to attack into the French rear starts a panic in the 55th Division sector. Heavy artillery units abandon their guns and flee. Other units retreat 5 miles toward the division headquarters. The 55th Infantry Division front collapses. The next day, XIX Panzerkorps captures 28 abandoned French artillery pieces. No German tanks cross the Meuse until the 14th.

9 By 2200hrs. The 1st Panzer Division infantry has captured Cheveuges and moved past the town. The 10th Panzer Division infantry has cleared the banks of the Meuse. It then clears the French main line of defence along the Marfée Heights overlooking Sedan. The 2nd Panzer Division has finally cleared French defences at Donchery and is moving units across by ferry. By nightfall on the 13th, the bridgehead is being expanded and fortified. Tank units will start moving across in the early morning of the 14th.

Sedan: 12–13 May

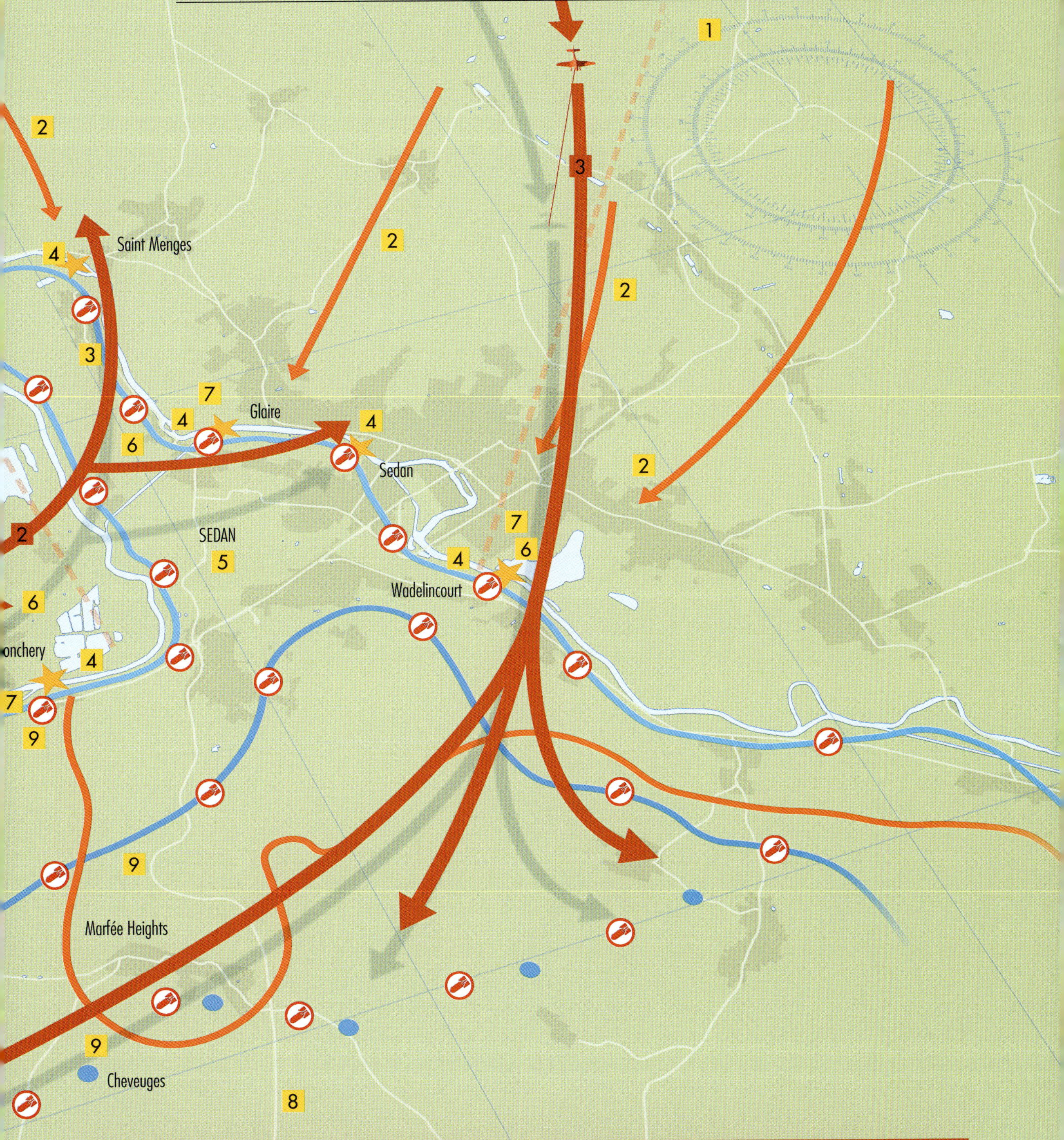

Saint Menges

Glaire

Sedan

SEDAN

Wadelincourt

onchery

Marfée Heights

Cheveuges

EVENTS IN THE AIR

1   13 May, 0700hrs. Luftwaffe reconnaissance planes fly over the French lines, noting all movement and activity.

2   0930hrs. The first Luftwaffe bombers and Stukas arrive and begin bombing the forward defence line (Stukas) and main defence lines and French artillery (Do 17, He 111, Ju 88 bombers). German bombing increases in intensity at 1100hrs.

3   1500hrs. Stukas stop their attacks on the bunkers of the French forward defence lines. They shift to bombing bunkers and strongpoints in the French main defence lines.

4   1700hrs. Luftflotte 3's bombardment of the French defenders stops. At this point, the XIX Panzerkorps has crossed the Meuse and has gone through the French forward defences.

the morning of the 14th Guderian ordered his tank units across. He wished to keep them together to hit the French with strong forces. The Panzer/air attack had torn a large hole in the French defence line of the Meuse and the XIXth Panzerkorps.

Luftflotte 3's air support for Guderian's assault across the Meuse on 13 May was the largest single air attack in history to that date. The Luftwaffe's Luftflotte 3, including part of the newly assigned VIII Fliegerkorps, committed 1,470 aircraft to the attack on 13 May. This amounted to almost 4,000 sorties, including many second sorties from the medium and light bombers. The Germans committed 600 medium and light bombers to the continuous carpet bombing of the main French defensive line. As groups arrived, each group of approximately 30 aircraft was directed to bomb assigned sectors, a squadron at a time. When that group finished, the next group would line up and repeat the process, then return to base to rearm for the next attack.

Similarly, 250 Ju 87s were employed to attack point targets along the river defences, squadron and group commanders sending in one flight at a time to attack targets and then return to base for the next attack. Five hundred Me 109s and 120 Me 110s were assigned close escort duties to cover and protect the bombers and Stukas from Allied fighters. Usually, a fighter group accompanied a bomber or Stuka group. As there was almost no Allied air activity to counter the Luftwaffe, the German fighters came in low and strafed the main French defensive lines in the rear areas. The French Second Army had only two battalions of obsolete World War I 75mm anti-aircraft guns for its whole front and had positioned one of them in the Sedan sector. However, the old guns posed little threat to the Luftwaffe and French anti-aircraft claimed only one German aircraft at Sedan on 13 May.

The French Second Army had some tank units attached that included heavily gunned and armoured Char B heavy tanks, more than a match for any German tank. French commanders considered an armoured counterattack against the German bridgehead at dawn on 14 May, well before a single German tank had crossed the Meuse, but caution got in the way. The French commanders decided to wait until they could organize full infantry and artillery support. By the time the French counterattack was ready, German armoured spearheads were moving quickly forward as French defensive effort petered out.

The battle over the bridgehead: Sedan, 14 May

The Allied High Command finally realized that the German crossing at Sedan was a crisis for the Allied army group. Allied attention shifted from the battles in Belgium and the southern Netherlands to the new threat to their centre. The French and British air forces agreed that Sedan was now a priority, and sent in every aircraft available to attack the bridgehead. Unlike fixed bridges across the Albert Canal, the pontoon bridges at Sedan were vulnerable to small bombs and strafing. Guderian's XIX Panzerkorps only began to move its tank units across the pontoon bridges at 0700hrs, and the XIX Panzerkorps' heavy combat units and support vehicles massed on the roads north of Sedan waiting to cross the bridges, presented an ideal target.

While the Germans had 303 anti-aircraft guns belonging to Luftwaffe Flak Regiment 102, and the flak battalions attached to the three Panzer divisions available to protect Guderian's Panzers, it would take time to get a strong flak force across the Meuse to set up an effective, 360-degree defence around the bridgehead. One can only surmise what might have occurred if the Allied air commanders had acted like Germans and committed 250 of Bomber Command's medium bombers to an early-morning raid to carpet bomb the entire bridge site. Such an attack would have seriously delayed Von Kleist and given the Allies a chance to mount a counterattack before the main body of XIXth Panzerkorps had crossed the Meuse.

Instead, French and British commanders relied on their own resources, although a few Blenheims from No. 2 Group from Britain were committed to the operation. RAF Bomber

RAF Blenheim No. 139 Squadron undergoing a routine engine overhaul in France in 1940. The well-trained RAF ground crew and technical NCOs ensured that the RAF squadrons in France had a high serviceability rate, much higher than l'Armée de l'Air, which lacked trained technical personnel.

Command remained reluctant to use its medium bombers in direct support for ground combat. The RAF Air Staff remained firmly convinced that using bombers to affect the ground battle was a misuse of aircraft.

The British response was to use its Fairey Battle light bombers in a series of small attacks in precisely the same way that the Battle bombers had been thrown away in attacking the bridges at Maastricht. The vulnerability of the German bridgehead in the morning of 14 May was evident. At dawn, six Battles of RAF No. 3 Squadron attacked the bridge site and returned, though one of the Battles was severely damaged and crashed on return. Another four Battles attacked at 0700hrs and managed to return. However, the French and British only managed to organize serious attacks in the afternoon when the situation at the Sedan bridgehead had

Ju 87s StG 77 bombing at Sedan, 13 May

As the Luftwaffe's most precise bomber, the Stuka played a key role in suppressing the French defences at Sedan on 13 May 1940. Sturzkampfgeschwader 77 (StG 77) had 75 operational dive bombers in two groups and was assigned to Generalmajor von Richthofen's VIII Fliegerkorps, which had been transferred from Luftflotte 2 to Luftflotte 3 on 12 May. Commander of StG 77 Oberst Günter Schwartzkopff, the Luftwaffe's leading dive-bomber expert, helped develop the Ju 87 Stuka and had developed Stuka tactics, which favoured diving from 9,000 to 10,000ft in a near-vertical angle.

Bombing of the French defences began at 0930hrs and Stuka squadrons lined up in flights of three aircraft to attack assigned targets. After bombing, the Stukas returned to their airfields to rearm and refuel for the next sortie. Most of StG 77's Stukas managed to fly three sorties at Sedan on 13 May, for a total of 201 sorties by the Geschwader.

This scene depicts Oberst Schwartzkopff leading his staff flight at 1100hrs observing his Stukas bombing French forward defences near the village of Donchery across from the 2nd Panzer Division's crossing point. Nine thousand feet below, the Stukas have just dropped their bombs as Schwartzkopff approaches his own target. While the bunkers were difficult to destroy with direct hits, some were damaged and by 1100hrs the French 55th Division infantry holding the trenches between the bunkers were already retreating, being totally unnerved by the Stuka attacks. The Luftwaffe's bombing enabled the XIX Panzerkorps to cross the Meuse at 1500hrs and quickly break through the forward and main French defence lines by early evening.

Schwartzkopff had been selected for promotion and to become the Luftwaffe Inspector of Stukas, but the next day he was shot down, either by anti-aircraft guns or an RAF Hurricane, in the Sedan area.

British soldiers in 1940 manning a 3in. heavy anti-aircraft gun. While the British Army had recently fielded a new and very effective 3.7in. anti-aircraft gun, most of the heavy anti-aircraft guns with the BEF were these obsolete World War I vintage weapons. (Alamy)

dramatically changed. German tank units were pushing the French farther back from the Meuse, and the Germans had time to organize a dense ring of flak guns around the bridges. Luftflotte 3 ordered Jagdgeschwader 27 to maintain a standing patrol by a fighter group over Sedan. What was to follow was a disaster for the Allied air forces.

The first major attack came at midday from the French Air Force, which sent in four LeO 451 modern bombers and 13 of the old Amiot 143s to bomb the bridgehead, with a close fighter escort. Of the 21 bombers, three Amiots and one LeO were lost. Guderian noted that though the bridges had not been hit, the air attacks caused delays for the crossings at Sedan.

The main British attack came at 1500hrs when 45 Battles attacked the German bridges and 15 Blenheims targeted the backed-up German columns. Five Battles of No. 12 Squadron dive-bombed the bridge into a wall of German 37mm and 20mm light flak; only one returned. Eight Battles of No. 142 Squadron attacked the bridges; four were lost. Of six Battles of No. 226 Squadron, three were lost and a fourth returned heavily damaged. No. 105 Squadron committed 11 Battles, and four returned. No. 150 Squadron lost all four of its Battles. No. 218 Squadron sent 11 Battles; only one returned. In total, the AASF had sortied 63 Battles to Sedan, and 35 had been lost. Five of the eight Blenheims sent out were lost. All returning Amiots had been damaged, most so badly that they were written off. The bomber force had been damaged so severely that the planned second attack was ruled out. The loss rate, more than 50%, makes it the worst day in RAF history.

Guderian admitted that French and British bomber attacks caused serious delays to the XIXth Panzerkorps, but the French Second Army had failed to take advantage of this. The French 21st Mechanized Corps contained some powerful tank units, including the French Char B heavy tank, which outclassed all Guderian's tanks. On 14 May, the 21st Mechanized Corps was ordered to attack the weakly held southern flank of the bridgehead. Yet General Huntziger delayed his counterattack until 15 May. By then, the 10th Panzer Division had fully crossed the Meuse and was ready. That day, the VIII Fliegerkorps' Stukas attacked the 21st Corps' supply and support vehicles, causing the French further delays.

The Sedan battle indicates just how effective Germany's Luftwaffe and army flak units could be as part of a joint warfare team. Luftwaffe Flak Regiment 102 remained attached to the XIX Panzerkorps throughout the campaign across France. The German flak force was not only effective in shooting down Allied aircraft, but also very effective when used against Allied armoured vehicles and in reducing concrete fortifications with direct fire. The Flak Regiment 102 was credited with 243 Allied aircraft destroyed during the campaign in France, almost half of the total aircraft credited to the German flak forces.

The disastrous attacks of 14 May came as a blow to Air Marshals Playfair and Barratt. The Battles, however, had not been knocked out of the fight, although the RAF would now use them far more cautiously. On 15 May, no missions were flown by the Battle squadrons, and on 15–16 May, the RAF in France began to retreat to airfields in the Troyes area in fear that the German armoured forces would turn south. Instead, the Germans continued west towards the Channel. The RAF's precipitous retreat led a considerable amount of equipment to be abandoned. The RAF's movement to airfields farther south was slowed by the roads, congested with retreating French Army forces and civilian refugees. However, the RAF had plenty of Battles in reserve, and the losses of the 14th were quickly replaced. By 19 May, seven Battle squadrons were available for operations.

The German drive from Sedan to the Channel

With Guderian's XIX Panzerkorps successfully crossing the Meuse on 13 and 14 May, along with another successful crossing of the Meuse by General Hoth's Panzerkorps at Dinant, on Guderian's right flank, the Germans would spend 14 and 15 May enlarging and consolidating a now sizeable bridgehead across the Meuse and repelling several French counterattacks.

Bomber force of Luftflotte 3 now turned its attention south and began conducting a series of large-scale attacks in group strength or more against French railyards and junctions throughout north-eastern France, and even south of the Aisne River, to delay any major French troop movements that might threaten Panzergruppe von Kleist. The short-range Stukas continued close air support of Panzergruppe von Kleist and Hoth's Panzerkorps, which provided effective support and demoralized the French defenders. However, the

A German light flak gun in 1940. (AC)

Stukas' close support could also have tragic consequences, and on the 14th, a squadron from Sturzkampfgeschwader 77 mistakenly bombed part of the 1st Panzer Division, killing a colonel and several key staff officers. Still, the German plan was far more successful than even the German High Command had hoped.

The halt order for Von Kleist

The German High Command became extremely nervous over the possibility of a major Allied counterattack that would separate Von Kleist's Panzer divisions from the follow-on infantry divisions that would move up behind and secure the German flank. The fear was that the infantry divisions, which were not motorized, would fall so far behind the Panzer advance that a large open flank would create an opportunity for the Allies. It was a reasonable understanding, as the German senior commanders had all served in the Great War and remembered how the Allies had managed to defeat major German tactical breakthroughs by a combination of effective defence and powerful counterattacks. Thus, on 16 May, even as Von Kleist and Hoth were pushing their reconnaissance and tank units west, the High Command ordered Von Kleist to halt the advance to enable supporting infantry divisions to catch up. This order was given even though no serious Allied defences were before them.

Advance to the Channel

On 15–16 May, the Luftwaffe began moving into captured airfields close to the front in western Belgium. The Luftwaffe engineer, airfield, and motorized supply companies were able to make the airfields serviceable in a day. Operating close to the front, the short-range Ju 87s and Henschel Hs 123s, along with their Bf 109E escorts, could routinely fly four sorties in a day and, on days of especially intense combat, could manage up to six sorties.

At a commanders' conference of the High Command on 16 May, the German High Command cited that the operational pause would soon be lifted. Generalmajor von Richthofen asserted that his VIII Fliegerkorps could provide flank protection to Von Kleist's Panzergruppe, and that his Stukas and Dornier light bombers would be able to spot and then attack any large Allied formations moving to engage Von Kleist's Panzer and motorized divisions. This bought time for the slow-moving infantry divisions to move up and defend the flanks. Von Richthofen's proposal was accepted, and orders issued to Von Rundstedt's army group to again begin the advance as rapidly as possible to the French coast on

A rear view taken by an RAF Fairey Battle of a German column in May 1940. The RAF and French Air Force also made troop movements a priority target. (IWM)

18 May. However, Guderian's XIX Panzerkorps, in the lead of Von Kleist's group, managed a considerable advance on 17 May by calling his movement a 'reconnaissance in force'.

Von Richthofen's proposal to use airpower to protect the flank of an armoured advance was a revolutionary move in terms of modern warfare. Von Richthofen had the advantage of having his FLIVO air liaison teams assigned to each of the armoured and motorized divisions, which meant that he would get constant reports regarding the ground and air situation throughout the day, as well as reports from the army units. Von Richthofen flew around the front in a Fieseler Fi 156 Storch, landing at forward headquarters and conferring with the senior commanders. Von Richthofen's orders from the Luftflotte 3 gave the VIII Fliegerkorps its first priority, to defend Panzergruppe von Kleist's flanks, and its second priority, to provide close air support to the forward units.

During the advance, Von Richthofen ordered that one Stuka group as well as one Bf 109 group be constantly available and ready for immediate take-off the moment that any significant Allied ground movement was spotted. The German practice of co-locating the Fliegerkorps forward command post alongside the supported army commander meant that, as situations arose, Von Richthofen or his chief of staff could immediately confer with the ground commander or his chief of staff and issue orders for an immediate strike. Within 45–75 minutes of the ground commander's requesting an air strike, a group of 30 Stukas and their escort fighters would arrive to put fire and steel on the target. In 1940, this was an amazingly quick, responsive system of close air support. In contrast, the Allied system had ground commanders put in a request for air support, which was passed up to army group headquarters, then passed on to the RAF and d'Astier's ZOAN headquarters, where requests were reviewed and air support priorities allocated. Perhaps several hours, or an entire day later, a small force of light bombers and escorting fighters would finally show up. Often, promised air support arrived long after the battle with German units no longer concentrated, but now dispersed in battle formations, making them a much harder target to find and bomb.

The failure of the British and French air attacks at Sedan on 14 May came as a shock to British and French air commanders. With his Battle light bomber force shot to pieces in the first five days of the campaign, Air Marshal Barratt pulled his Battles out of the fight, as he rested and reequipped his depleted bomber force.

Barratt's order to redeploy RAF units south put several squadrons out of the battle as RAF ground crew abandoned their airfields and left behind equipment and dozens of damaged aircraft that could not be quickly repaired.

French counterattacks stymied by the Luftwaffe
On 11 May, Colonel Charles de Gaulle assumed command of the French 4th Armoured Division. Still in the process of being formed, de Gaulle's 4th Armoured Division consisted of several powerful tank battalions, but only one infantry battalion, and no artillery or support troops. Nonetheless, attempting to stall Von Kleist's advance, on 17 May de Gaulle began a 20-mile advance into the flank of the 10th Panzer Division and seized the important crossroads at Montcornet. De Gaulle had requested strong air support for his advance but received only a paltry dozen aircraft. Still, de Gaulle made it to Montcornet, having overrun a couple of German columns on the way. At Montcornet, the 10th Panzer Division rushed up anti-tank guns and blocking forces and counterattacked. The 4th Armoured Division's one infantry battalion was not enough to hold the gains the tanks had made, so de Gaulle was forced to withdraw. At this point, the VIII Fliegerkorps' Stukas arrived to attack de Gaulle's retreating forces, targeting his supply and fuel trucks.

On the 19th, de Gaulle's 4th Armoured Division launched an attack at Crécy-sur-Serre again into Von Kleist's flank. This time, the 4th Armoured Division was reinforced by more tanks and a battalion of 75mm guns for artillery support, yet it still had only a single infantry battalion. This time, General d'Astier promised more air support, but due to poor

German 20mm flak gun guarding a rail bridge in Belgium, May 1940. The Luftwaffe deployed enough modern flak guns in spring 1940 to ensure that not only were the front-line units protected from air attack, but there were enough guns to spare to put strong anti-aircraft defences around key targets such as bridges. (AC)

army-air coordination, the promised air support only arrived after de Gaulle's attack was again stymied by a hasty German defence line. De Gaulle again withdrew his division under heavy air attack by VIII Fliegerkorps Stukas, and the promised air support only appeared after his force was withdrawn.

On 18 May, Von Rundstedt's army group, with Von Kleist in the centre and flanked on the right by the 4th Army's Panzer and motorized corps, began the final stage of the advance to the Channel. Advancing up to 30 miles a day, the German massed Panzer and motorized forces found the Allied rear to be disorganized, with French regiments and divisions in the path of the Germans unaware of the Panzer forces until they were overrun. In the meantime, Von Richthofen patrolled the flanks with Do 17Z long-range reconnaissance aircraft to spot Allied columns within 30 miles of the German front and call for Stukas to attack any large French formations.

The Luftwaffe's campaign had become a close-run thing in terms of logistics. The rapid German armoured advances in Poland and the Luftwaffe's ability to establish forward airfields in short order had only been possible by using the Luftwaffe's fleet of 500 Ju 52 transports. In addition to transports flying in loads of fuel, bombs, and personnel to set up forward airfields, in Poland there were enough aircraft to fly fuel to supply Panzer divisions that had outrun their supply lines. However, the first days of the campaign in the Netherlands had decimated the transport force, and of the 500 transports available at the start of the campaign, half had been destroyed or badly damaged, leaving only 200 aircraft to support the needs of the army and Panzer forces. Luckily for Von Kleist and the German Panzer and motorized divisions, captured French fuel stocks enabled German armour to continue the attack, though by 19 May the forward divisions had little more than a day's fuel left. Von Richthofen's Stukas and fighters were able to carry out four or more sorties a day because a large British fuel dump near Arras had been captured and had not only ample stocks of gasoline, but also aviation fuel. Despite logistics problems, on the night of 20 May, Von Kleist's spearhead reached the English Channel near Abbeville and severed the BEF and the French 1st and 7th Armies from the rest of the French Army. The French Ninth Army had been shattered by German Panzers and its remnants were being reformed.

Since 14 May, the RAF battle force was basically out of action. The fighter component of the RAF had lost half of the 200 Hurricanes that had been sent to France. On 14 May, d'Astier's ZOAN fighter force had flown 340 sorties, but on 15 May, air activity was severely reduced and d'Astier had no more than 237 serviceable fighters, 38 night fighters, and only 38 bombers on his northern front. On 15 May, the French flew only 200 fighter sorties.

On 15 May, the Allied armies in Belgium, which had been holding German Generaloberst Fedor von Bock's Army Group B, were in retreat across the whole front. The RAF had not only taken the Battles out of combat, but on the 15th only eight Blenheim sorties were flown, four for reconnaissance. The main focus of the AASF that day was to provide patrols to protect the French First Army, engaged in western Belgium.

Even as the German High Command called for a halt of their Panzer advance at Sedan, the situation in Belgium became worse. The surrender of the Netherlands on 14 May compelled the French Seventh Army to pull back, and Air Marshal Barratt and BEF Commander Lord Gort urgently requested that more fighter squadrons be deployed from the UK. The War Cabinet quickly approved sending four more squadrons to France immediately, with two more to follow. Yet the War Cabinet was also confronted with a letter from Air Marshal Dowding, chief of RAF Fighter Command, arguing that the RAF was in danger of compromising the minimum fighter force, calculated at 36 squadrons, required to defend British airspace. A compromise was reached in which the RAF in France would be reinforced by flights or half-squadrons sent from Britain, while other British squadrons would be sent from the bases in England to fly with the AASF in the morning and return to the UK in the evening.

Britain and France had fighters that could be committed to the northern front, but the bombing of Rotterdam on 14 May had highlighted the danger to French and British cities. General Gamelin was not prepared to strip the fighter defences around Paris in the same way that Dowding was unwilling to strip fighters from the defence of England. So, hundreds of fighters were held back from the great battle in the north and the Luftwaffe would hold a better than 2:1 superiority in fighter aircraft during the decisive battle for France.

A Bf 109 group operating from a captured airfield in June 1940. (AC)

OPPOSITE BOMBER COMMAND BASES

Bomber Command responds

The German bombing of Rotterdam took place in the last moments of the German campaign for the Netherlands. German airborne forces dropped on 10 May had managed – barely – to hold on to a key bridgehead at Rotterdam, allowing the German Panzer forces a path to conquer the last part of the Dutch final defensive lines. On the morning of 14 May, having evacuated the Dutch king and government leaders to England the day before, the Dutch had already begun talks with the Germans to surrender the Dutch Army in the Netherlands. The Germans had threatened that Rotterdam would be heavily bombed if the Dutch did not surrender immediately.

The fact that the Dutch had indicated a willingness to surrender caused Generalleutnant Student, the German commander on the spot, to call off Luftflotte 2's bomber attack. Yet the first wave, consisting of 54 bombers from KG 54, was already approaching the target and failed to receive the signal to abort. In total 97 tons of bombs fell on Rotterdam, gutting much of the medieval city centre, causing large fires, and killing approximately 900 civilians. The follow-on bomber waves got the message and returned to their bases, and the Dutch surrender proceeded.

The bombing of Rotterdam incited headlines around the world as an example of ruthless Nazi terror bombing. British, American, and European newspapers reported that the bomb raid had not only levelled Rotterdam, but had killed 20,000 civilians. Exaggerating the threat of German bombers to Allied cities ensured that the British and French governments retained considerable fighter forces to defend their cities.

From the start of the war, it had been British policy not to bomb German cities, and the few raids that had taken place such as the RAF raid on the German naval base at Wilhelmshaven at the start of the war had resulted in such heavy losses that daylight raids against Germany, far beyond the range of any escort fighters, could not be considered. But after Rotterdam, RAF Bomber Command insisted that its most effective response to the ground battle in Belgium and France was a night-bombing campaign against German cities.

The British bombing offensive

Despite the aerial debacle at Sedan and the bombing of Rotterdam, both on 14 May, the RAF decided in accordance with their ingrained pre-war concepts that the strategic bomber offensive was the best use of Bomber Command. The RAF staff decided a bombing campaign would so damage German industry in the Ruhr, especially the oil refineries at Mönchengladbach, that the Luftwaffe would be compelled to withdraw fighter units from France and Belgium. The first raid against German cities came in the night of 15–16 May when 100 medium Wellington and Hampden bombers attacked 16 targets in the Ruhr cities. Each target was allocated from five to nine aircraft. As British night-flying training had been especially weak before the war, only 24 bomber crews found their intended targets. The rest of the bombers attacked any target of opportunity. Initial pilot reports enthusiastically described great fireballs and secondary explosions from the targets hit. In fact, the damage was minor and the German High Command had no realization that it was receiving a major bombing offensive. In the night of 17–18 May, Bomber Command sent 53 medium bombers to attack targets of opportunity between Dinant and Gembloux in Belgium, but the main effort that night was to send 72 bombers to the Ruhr, again in small attacks. Again, the main British target, namely the German oil industry at Mönchengladbach, received only minor damage, and the bombs dropped on Germany were so scattered that the German High Command thought the British were carrying out some kind of training operations with bombs added for realism.

Grangemouth
No 141 Sqn/*Blenheim, Battle*

North Sea

Dishforth
No 49 Sqn/*Whitley*

Linton-on-Ouse
No 58 Sqn/*Whitley*
No 78 Sqn/*Whitley*

Driffield
No 77 Sqd/*Whitley*
No 102 Sqn/*Whitley*

Helmswell
No 144 Sqn/*Hampden*
No 61 Sqn/*Hampden*

Finningsley
No 106 Sqn/*Hampden*

Scampton
No 83 Sqn/*Hampden*
No 49 Sqn/*Hampden*

Waddington
No 50 Sqn/*Hampden*

West Raynham
No 101 Sqn/*Blenheim*

Marham
No 115 Sqn/*Wellington*

Watton
No 82 Sqn/*Blenheim*

Feltwell
No 75 Sqn/*Wellington*

Mildenhall
No 149 Sqn/*Wellington*

Newmarket
No 99 Sqn/*Wellington*

Wattisham
No 107 Sqn/*Blenheim*
No 108 Sqn /*Blenheim*

BRITAIN

Stradishall
No 148 Sqn/*Wellington*

London

NETHERLANDS

BELGIUM

Calais

Brussels

Lille

FRANCE

Seine

Paris

N

0   50 miles

0   50km

The RAF attacked Hamburg and Bremen on 17 May and the only serious damage to the German economy was two warehouses full of furniture confiscated from Jews that were burned down. The Germans remained unimpressed with the British attacks and no aircraft were pulled out of the battle in France to defend the Fatherland.

After the Sedan breakthrough, both the British and French air forces were in a defensive mode, with only a few small and well-escorted missions conducted in daylight. Well-escorted bomber missions had a lower loss rate, as was shown by Bomber Command's No. 2 Group's missions on 15 May. Twelve unescorted Blenheims were sent out and three lost, while another mission of 12 Blenheims escorted by French Curtiss Hawk fighters took no losses. On 17 May, 12 Blenheims attacked the Germans at Gembloux, Belgium, but missed their escorts, and all but one was shot down. On 18 May, six Blenheims were sent on missions, and three were lost. On 17 May, RAF Air Component Lysanders and Blenheims were sent into battle to attack German columns at Le Cateau and Saint-Quentin with some success. Yet, by this time, it was clear that small bombing raids, even escorted by fighters, did little to the German advance.

Barratt's RAF component and d'Astier's fighter force had their main priority to the French Army with fighter protection against the Stukas. RAF Hurricanes were sent out daily to fly patrols over areas of heavy combat where the army requested air support. French and British fighters often ran into large German raids, generally bomber or Stuka groups escorted by a full group of Bf 109s and 110s. Although Allied fighters were usually outnumbered in the fight, they took a steady toll on the Germans. What was especially disruptive to the French and British air forces were the repeated heavy attacks against Allied airfields. On 18 May, Heinkel 111s of I/KG 54 attacked the Amiens-Glisy Aerodrome, the main RAF airfield for receiving replacement Hurricanes and Blenheims. That same day, Vitry Airfield, where RAF 61 Fighter Wing was stationed, was forced to defend its airfield from two major German attacks from Bf 110s of I/ZG 26, Ju 88s of III/LG 1, and three squadrons of Dornier Do 17s from III/KG 76. The Germans lost three Bf 110s, but seven Hurricanes, four Gladiators, and one Blenheim were all destroyed on the ground, and other aircraft were badly damaged.

18 May saw extensive patrolling by RAF Hurricanes over Lille. It was a bad day for the RAF, as 22 Hurricanes were shot down by the Germans in battles over their airfields, and another 13 made forced landings with heavy damage. RAF Merville airfield was attacked twice, with serious damage to the aircraft on the ground.

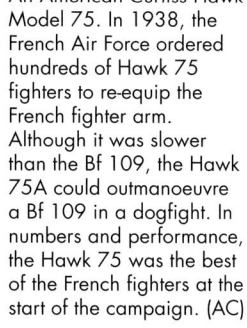

An American Curtiss Hawk Model 75. In 1938, the French Air Force ordered hundreds of Hawk 75 fighters to re-equip the French fighter arm. Although it was slower than the Bf 109, the Hawk 75A could outmanoeuvre a Bf 109 in a dogfight. In numbers and performance, the Hawk 75 was the best of the French fighters at the start of the campaign. (AC)

D'Astier responded to French Army demands to put fighters over the ground troops. There were a few attempts to provide ground support as the French lacked an established method for coordinating air strikes with the army. French bombers and escort fighters were given general targets, but not specific targets. Colonel de Gaulle's first attack at Montcornet on 17 May, despite initial progress, was denied air support, which was crucial since the 4th Armoured Division had no artillery. Instead, d'Astier diverted his few modern bombers to support the First North African Division in heavy combat nearby. In all 18 ground-strafing Potez 631 fighters and 12 LeO 451 bombers were sent to help the French Army, but no escort was provided for the LeO bombers and four of the bombers were shot down. On 16 May, one small mission by the LeO 451s received an escort of 24 Bloch fighters, yet on the 17th, d'Astier informed General Vuillemin that the burden of escorting daylight bombers took up far too much of his fighter force, and asked Vuillemin for permission to stop using his fighters as escorts, even though this would mean that his bombers could only conduct night missions.

Spring 1940. Battle bombers of RAF No. 88 Squadron escorted by Hawk 75s of Combat Group GC 1/2 of the French Air Force. Air Commanders Air Marshal Barratt and General d'Astier, worked to ensure mutual cooperation between the two air forces.

French naval dive bombers attack the Panzer advance at Berlaimont, France, 18 May

18 May was a day of desperate ground and aerial combat as the German Panzer divisions pushed west to the Channel. The French Northern Air Zone (ZOAN) had operational command of six squadrons of the French Naval Air Arm (72 aircraft) based on the Channel coast; four of these squadrons were Navy dive bombers. From 14–18 May, the dive-bomber squadrons had been busy supporting the French Seventh Army retreat from the Netherlands. The dive bombers had flown 50 sorties and only once encountered German flak defences. But they had yet to encounter Panzer divisions, each of which had a full battalion of motorized flak guns attached.

The crossroads of two highways met at the small town of Berlaimont, France, near the Belgian border, and the 7th and 5th Panzer Divisions were using the crossroads. It was an ideal target for French bombers to damage and disrupt the German advance. Aware of this, the 7th Panzer Division emplaced at least two batteries of light flak guns (24 guns) to cover the crossroads. The light flak was exceptionally lethal for low-flying aircraft.

Two French Navy dive-bomber squadrons, AB2 and AB4, each with ten aircraft, were detailed to attack the crossroads. The squadrons flew the Loire-Nieuport LN.401 and LN.411 dive bombers (essentially the same aircraft with small variations). The Loire-Nieuports were far less capable than the Ju 87, whose 1,200hp engine enabled it to carry 1,100lb of bombs. The Loire-Nieuports had 690hp engines and had only a 500lb bombload. While good in a dive, the Loire-Nieuports were very slow, with a maximum speed of 240mph and a cruise speed of 186mph.

The dive bombers, led by French Navy Lieutenant Francis Lainé, commander of AB4, took off from Berck Airfield on the Channel coast in the early evening and flew a direct course to Berlaimont, which took them 50 miles over German-held territory. German Army units spotted the bombers and gave warning to the Panzer divisions near Berlaimont.

Instead of diving from high altitude like the German Stukas, Lieutenant Lainé decided to fly in at low level – 1,800–2,000ft, for maximum accuracy. But slow aircraft flying a straight course at 2,000ft made a perfect target for the 20 and 37mm flak guns. As the attack began at 1900hrs, Lieutenant Lainé was flying the lead aircraft depicted here. His aircraft was damaged, but he dropped his bomb and managed to return. His two wingmen were hit at the start of the bomb run, one being destroyed.

Of the 20 planes on the mission, 11 were shot down by German flak near Berlaimont. One aircraft was shot down by French anti-aircraft guns as it returned to base. One was lost to a German fighter. Of the seven aircraft that returned, six were so badly damaged by flak that they were no longer flyable. At the end of the day, the two squadrons could field only one serviceable aircraft. While the surviving French Navy pilots reported heavy damage to the Germans, the actual damage was light and imposed little delay to the Panzer divisions.

With Vuillemin's approval, on 18 May d'Astier's dwindling fighter force was committed to flying patrols along the front and patrolling the rail lines from Paris to protect the movement of army reinforcements. This strategy had moderate success, with Curtiss Hawk fighters of GC I/5 and Hawks of GC II/4 with Moranes from GC II/2 engaging a group of Heinkels, shooting down five of the He 111s and two Bf 109s.

On 19 May, the day of de Gaulle's second major attack, the LeO bombers that were to attack German formations near de Gaulle saw their airfield bombed and most of the group's bombers destroyed on the ground. Due to poor communications, the fighters to protect de Gaulle's Fourth Armoured Division arrived late. De Gaulle's initial success was stopped by an improvised line of German flak and artillery, and especially by the rapid arrival of a Stuka group, which inflicted heavy casualties on the French infantry and support vehicles.

To the north, d'Astier committed 20 French Navy Loire-Nieuport LN 411 dive bombers of squadrons AB2 through AB4 to attack German Panzer forces at Berlaimont, which had an important crossroads required by the advancing 5th and 7th Panzer Divisions. The Panzer columns were backed up on the road at Berlaimont, making an enticing target.

The naval dive bombers had been operating in the Netherlands in support of the French Seventh Army and had flown several missions without loss. They were apparently confident of their ability to hit the target. They were supposed to be escorted by Navy Potez 631 fighters, but owing to miscommunication, they missed their rendezvous. The Loire-Nieuport dive bombers flew a course that took them 50 miles over German-held territory to their target. FLIVOs and German Army units gave a warning of French aircraft in their vicinity and, knowing the crossroads were a key position, dozens of flak guns surrounded the target. French dive bombers went in at low altitude to ensure accuracy, but a low-altitude approach was also ideal for the German light flak, highly lethal up to 4,000ft, but less lethal against a high-altitude dive-bombing approach. In moments, eight attacking dive bombers were shot down. The survivors made bomb runs, but all returned with heavy damage. A ninth damaged dive bomber was shot down on its return leg by an Me 109, and a tenth dive bomber was mistakenly identified as a German aircraft and shot down by French anti-aircraft fire. It was a 50% loss rate for the mission and, of the two squadrons, only one aircraft was flyable the next day.

As the Germans reached the Channel, the consequences of the German advance forced the Allied High Command to understand the crisis. On 18 May, the French government relieved military Commander-in-Chief General Gamelin and replaced him with General Maxime Weygand, who had been the French military commander in the Near East.

On the 19th, the RAF ordered the air component of the BEF and the remnants of the AASF to evacuate to England. Over the next two days, all flyable aircraft were flown to south-east England, and RAF airfields in northern France were evacuated. Damaged or unserviceable aircraft at the RAF's northern French airbases were destroyed, and RAF aircrew were left to transport themselves to French ports and get back to England. From 10 to 20 May, the RAF lost 200 Hurricanes in France and Belgium. As an additional blow, 178 British aircraft had to be destroyed as unserviceable.

The BEF and General Billotte's army group were directed to organize a major attack on the German flanks to break the German encirclement. On 21 May, Lord Gort was only able to assemble a small force for what should have been at least a two-division attack. The French First Army had taken heavy losses; its morale was breaking, and it was unable to support an attack. The only French support were some tank units from the French Cavalry Corps.

The British attacked the German flank at Arras on the afternoon of 21 May. The 54 British Matilda heavy tanks drove deep into the German lines, overrunning the infantry of General Hoth's Panzer Corps. It soon became clear that the Matilda's armour – the thickest armour on the battlefield in 1940 – was impervious to the anti-tank guns of the Panzer divisions. The British attack drove ten miles into the German lines, overran two German columns, and inflicted heavy casualties, until it was slowed by an improvised defence line of artillery and 88mm anti-aircraft guns, the only German guns capable of piercing the Matilda's armour.

Neither General Billotte nor Lord Gort was able to coordinate any air strikes with General d'Astier, so the British attack went in with no air support. But after the initial British breakthrough, Luftflotte 2 Stukas arrived and slowed down the British armoured advance, separating the tanks from their supporting infantry. Without follow-on forces to exploit the success, the British withdrew, having conducted what was a successful raid that would nonetheless only briefly delay the Panzer divisions moving to encircle the Allied forces at Arras.

General Weygand decided to meet with the Allied commanders, now isolated in the north, and coordinate a large-scale breakout offensive. He had a suspenseful flight from Paris to Calais, when his transport plane was fired upon by German anti-aircraft and attacked by Bf 109 fighters. When Weygand finally arrived in Calais, he was driven to Ypres, where he met with the Belgian king and General Billotte. Lord Gort was unavailable as he was trying to coordinate more support for the Arras attack. Weygand received a thoroughly pessimistic view of the Belgian Army and a discouraging report from General Billotte, who explained the heavy losses his forces had taken and their breaking morale. Weygand returned to Paris and tried to organize an offensive to break the German encirclement, but of the Allied forces in Belgium and northern France, only the BEF divisions appeared capable of further effort. Lord Gort understood that the only hope to save the BEF was evacuation through Dunkirk, so the military situation required a speedy withdrawal. The British pulled back 15 miles from Arras with a plan to withdraw to Dunkirk over the next days.

In the meantime, after reaching the Channel on 20 May, the Germans had an operational pause. Von Kleist's divisions reached the Channel short of fuel, and had lost a significant part of their tank force, less through enemy action than the mechanical breakdowns bound to occur after two weeks of non-stop movement and combat. The Luftwaffe had its own logistics difficulties, as the VIII Fliegerkorps was in the process of shifting its Stukas and fighters to Saint-Pol, close to Flanders and within range of the Channel cities. One boon for the German supply situation was the capture at Arras of a vast Allied supply depot containing large stocks of gasoline and aviation fuel that was commandeered to fuel Stukas and escort fighters.

The campaign over Dunkirk

Von Kleist's preference when reaching the Channel coast on 20 May was to quickly advance his forces along the coast to seize the ports of Boulogne, Calais, and Dunkirk. However, the German Army and Luftwaffe were also in the process of regrouping and reorganizing their forces for the upcoming Battle of France, called *Fall Rot* (Case Red) by the Germans. The German High Command began planning for the final campaign against France on 20 May and the priority for the German Army groups was to seize bridgeheads across the Somme and Aisne rivers and to redeploy German Panzer forces to spearhead the final offensive into France. Army Group B, with its left flank at Abbeville, would advance on the western flank and Army Group A would cross the Aisne River east of Paris and drive south.

The final offensive would begin on 5 June, and the reduction of the Belgian-French BEF forces being pushed into Flanders would now be left to Army Group B, supported by Luftflotte 2 and its four air corps. From the south, Guderian's XIX Panzerkorps, supported by Von Richthofen's VIII Fliegerkorps, continued to advance up the Channel coast to seize Boulogne, Calais, and Dunkirk, the last ports on the French coast that could serve as evacuation points for the Allied armies.

Even as the British were attacking at Arras on 21 May, the British High Command sent brigades from England to garrison both Boulogne and Calais. The British units disembarked at Calais and Boulogne on 22 May, quickly establishing defence perimeters. The XIX

Panzerkorps received permission to advance along the Channel coast on 22 May with parts of three Panzer divisions. Elements of the 2nd Panzer Division and forward columns of the 1st and 10th Panzer Divisions arrived at Calais by the evening of the 22nd. The brief pause in German operations allowed the British to turn Calais and Boulogne into bastions that would require considerable effort by the Germans to overcome. The main part of the BEF did not begin its retreat from Arras until 23 May, and would have to travel a considerable distance to Dunkirk.

True to the German Army and Luftwaffe's manner of command, Von Richthofen flew to visit General Guderian on 21 May, and over dinner, Guderian briefed his plans for attacking north and Von Richthofen explained to Guderian what support the VIII Fliegerkorps could provide. The two generals agreed on a plan to attack Boulogne and Calais. The siege of Boulogne and Calais began on 23 May, with the 2nd Panzer Division attacking Boulogne and the 10th Panzer attacking Calais. In the meantime, other elements of the XIX Panzerkorps advanced on the 23rd to the River Aa. Dunkirk was only 22 miles away and German armoured forces were in a position to overrun Dunkirk with little to stop them.

Fate intervened to save the Allied armies in the person of Reichsmarschall Göring. At a staff meeting in Berlin on 23 May, Göring had declared that his Luftwaffe alone could handle the final destruction of the Allied armies, while the Panzer forces could rest and regroup for the next stage of the campaign. It was typical of the bombastic and corrupt Reichsmarschall to make such fateful strategic decisions without consulting either the army or the air commanders on the ground. The air fleet and air corps commanders were surprised by Göring's order. The Luftwaffe, for its part, was short on supplies including fuel and munitions, and had taken heavy losses over the previous two weeks. Losses amounted to approximately 25% of units such as the VIII Fliegerkorps and had not yet been fully replaced. Most of the Luftwaffe units were understrength and the fighter and Stuka units were based at overcrowded captured French and Belgian airfields and were short of stores of fuel and munitions.

Such was the decision-making in the Third Reich that Hitler accepted Göring's declaration and issued a Führerbefehl – that is, a Führer order – to halt any forward movement of Von

An Allied troop column caught on the road near Dunkirk in May 1940. The British and French evacuation to Dunkirk left a trail of destroyed vehicles through northern France and Belgium, victims of Luftwaffe attacks. (AC)

Kleist's troops on 24 May. This decision, along with the decision to reinforce the Channel ports, gave Lord Gort just enough time to organize a retreat of the BEF. A defence perimeter was established around Dunkirk by the 27th, with much of the Allied front protected by canals and flooded regions, impassable to ground troops.

In the meantime, Army Group B – confronting Belgian BEF forces in northern Belgium – had received no stop order, and the Belgians were being rapidly pushed backward, unable to hold any defence lines. But a factor that helped save the BEF and many French units was the staunch resistance of half the French First Army that had been surrounded in Lille. From 24 to 28 May, seven German divisions were tied up in the battle for Lille, where 35,000 French soldiers surrendered on 28 May. This gave the BEF divisions a brief period to withdraw to Dunkirk. This was the finest hour of the BEF, as a successful and orderly retreat under heavy pressure is an exceptionally difficult manoeuvre. The BEF III Corps, along with units of the French 7th and 1st Armies, were the first forces to arrive at the Dunkirk perimeter by the 27th. The BEF II Corps arrived from 28–30 May and the BEF I Corps arrived on 29 May. There had been no panic and, although now on half rations, the Allied forces in the pocket were still organized, cohesive units.

The air campaign over Dunkirk was an improvised operation for both sides. The Luftwaffe had the three Fliegerkorps of Kesselring's Luftflotte 2 (I, II, and IV Fliegerkorps), and Luftflotte 3's VIII Fliegerkorps was engaged. Altogether, this amounted to over 1,000 aircraft that could be brought against the Allied pocket. Yet, for the opening days of the Dunkirk operations, Luftflotte 2 and VIII Fliegerkorps had other priority missions. Von Richthofen's Stukas were busy supporting Guderian's Panzers in the siege of Boulogne and Calais until the British garrisons were forced to surrender on 26 May. The British had attempted to evacuate some of their troops from Boulogne, but the mechanized brigade and tank battalion that the British sent to Calais were ordered to fight and hold out, without any hope of evacuation, until resistance was impossible. This sacrifice was to buy time for the BEF to withdraw into the Dunkirk perimeter.

The sieges of Calais and Boulogne featured one of the recent innovations in Luftwaffe tactics that had come from the Polish campaign. In Poland, the Germans noted that the 500- and 1,000lb bombs of the Luftwaffe were not sufficient to destroy thick concrete and

Convoy of ships evacuating Allied troops from Dunkirk. (AC)

Dunkirk

The first major German air attack after Operation *Dynamo* begins on 27 May when Luftflotte 2 flies 225 bombers and 75 Stukas, with fighter escorts, against Dunkirk. Luftflotte 2 loses 24 aircraft, including ten He 111s, its worst day of losses ever. From 27 May to 3 June, Luftflotte 2 and VIII Fliegerkorps attack the Dunkirk perimeter whenever the weather is clear. There are 1,026 bomber sorties, 826 Stuka sorties and 1,997 fighter sorties.

Fighter Command's 11 Group under Air Marshal Parks has the mission of flying fighter cover for the evacuation. 11 Group has 16 fighter squadrons based in south-east England – about 200 fighters. In total, they fly 2,739 sorties. The Luftwaffe loses 100 aircraft and the RAF 106 fighters and 80 pilots.

RAF Fighter Patrol Area

Bray Dunes

DUNKIRK

Gravelines

EVENTS

1   23 May. Advance units of the 1st Panzer Division reach the Aa River/canal south of Dunkirk and are in position to drive on to Dunkirk. Hitler issues the order on 24 May to halt Von Kleist's advance.

2   26 May. Halt order lifted. Germans advance towards Dunkirk on 27–28 May. Gravelines falls to the Germans. Dunkirk city and harbour are now within the range of German heavy artillery.

3   27 May. A massive raid on Dunkirk's harbour devastates the inner harbour, which is now unuseable. Evacuations will have to embark using the harbour outer mole.

4   26–30 May. Retreat of the French Seventh Army and part of the First Army, also the three corps of the BEF move into Dunkirk. The BEF II Corps is first into the perimeter on the 26–27 May, followed by the III Corps on 28–30 May and the I Corps on 29–30 May.

5   27 May. Lord Gort sets up the BEF headquarters at the village of La Panne on the beach east of Dunkirk. A strong perimeter defence behind canals and flooded areas is manned by French forces and the British II Corps. The Dunkirk perimeter is divided into defence zones with the eastern zone to be held by BEF III Corps, the middle by the BEF II and I Corps, and Dunkirk and the western perimeter by the French Army.

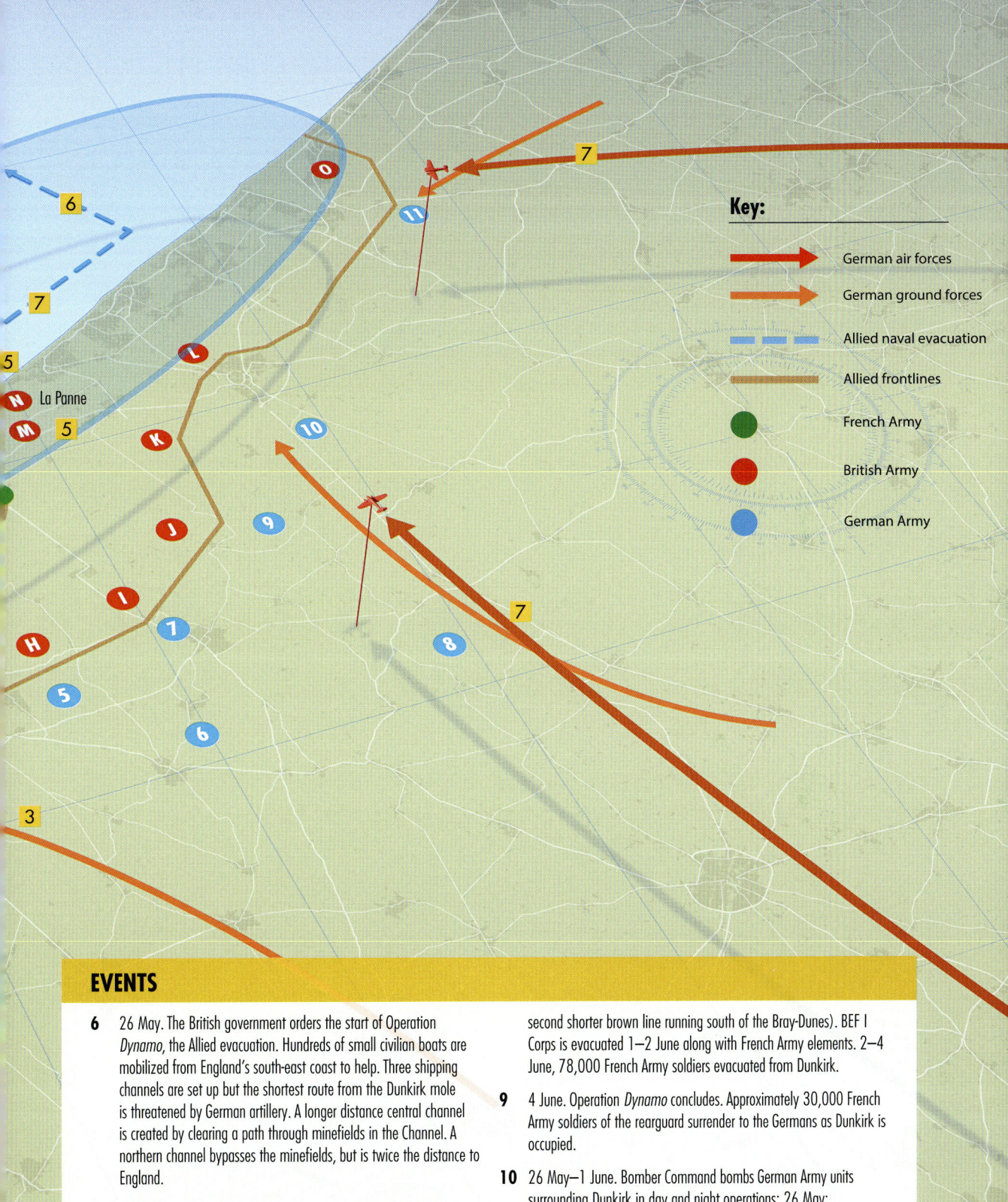

La Panne

EVENTS

6 26 May. The British government orders the start of Operation *Dynamo*, the Allied evacuation. Hundreds of small civilian boats are mobilized from England's south-east coast to help. Three shipping channels are set up but the shortest route from the Dunkirk mole is threatened by German artillery. A longer distance central channel is created by clearing a path through minefields in the Channel. A northern channel bypasses the minefields, but is twice the distance to England.

7 1 June. The day of the heaviest ship losses for the Allies. Three Royal Navy destroyers: HMS *Basilisk*, HMS *Havant* and HMS *Keith* are sunk by Luftwaffe Stukas just off the beach at La Panne.

8 26–29 May. The evacuation of Dunkirk is done by commands: BEF rear troops and II Corps withdrawn 26–29 May; BEF III Corps withdrawn 30 May–1 June (the perimeter contracts on 1 June to the

second shorter brown line running south of the Bray-Dunes). BEF I Corps is evacuated 1–2 June along with French Army elements. 2–4 June, 78,000 French Army soldiers evacuated from Dunkirk.

9 4 June. Operation *Dynamo* concludes. Approximately 30,000 French Army soldiers of the rearguard surrender to the Germans as Dunkirk is occupied.

10 26 May–1 June. Bomber Command bombs German Army units surrounding Dunkirk in day and night operations: 26 May: 34 Blenheims, 27 May: 48 Blenheims, 28 May: 48 Blenheims by day, 13 Whitleys by night, 29 May: 51 Blenheims by day, 47 Whitleys and Wellingtons by night, 30 May: 68 Blenheims, due to poor weather only 44 bombs, 31 May: 28 Wellingtons, Night 31 May–1 June: 126 Bomber sorties, 1 June: 56 Blenheims.

An Allied ship that took a direct hit from a Ju 87 Stuka. (AC)

masonry fortifications. So, in October 1939, the Luftwaffe began developing an armour-piercing, 1,000lb bomb with a delayed fuse that would explode the bomb a fraction of a second after impact. This would allow a heavy bomb to pierce through layers of concrete and masonry before exploding, thus creating a far greater blast effect. By May 1940, the new bombs were ready for the Luftwaffe to use in the campaign.

In late May, Luftflotte 2 was committed to providing air support to Army Group B forces pursuing the Belgian Army, and Luftflotte 3 was engaged in supporting Army Group A at Lille where a large part of the French 1st Army was trapped. Belgium and its army would surrender on 28 May, giving little prior notice to its French and British allies.

With most of the BEF air component and AASF now evacuated, the BEF and French forces retreated to Dunkirk. Allied forces holding Calais and Boulogne received air support from 11 Group of Fighter Command, based in south-east England. After the Germans reached the Channel on 20 May, squadrons of 11 Group were within range to aggressively engage the Luftwaffe over the Channel ports. German airmen reported that for the first time since the start of the campaign, they no longer enjoyed air superiority over the battlefield. Now the Luftwaffe had its first combat with the RAF's Spitfire squadrons.

The battle for Dunkirk began on 25 May with a heavy bombardment of Dunkirk's inner harbour by Luftflotte 2 bombers. It was not the first raid that Dunkirk had experienced, but this particular raid caused such devastation to the inner harbour that it was rendered unuseable, so that any troop evacuation at Dunkirk would have to take place by British and French ships docking alongside the outer wall of Dunkirk harbour. The British government ordered Operation *Dynamo*, the evacuation of Allied forces from Dunkirk, to begin on 26 May. A major part of the operation consisted of the British action to assemble hundreds of small boats, including pleasure craft, motorboats, and sailboats, manned by civilian volunteers. Some of the small boats could take Allied personnel straight from the beaches and across the Channel to England. But the small craft were mostly useful for shuttling Allied soldiers straight from the miles of beaches along the coast out to larger ships anchored just off the beaches. The main effort to evacuate from the Dunkirk Outer Mole was supported by Royal Navy destroyers as well as French Navy destroyers.

The largest German attack against Dunkirk was carried out on 27 May, when Luftflotte 2 dispatched 225 bombers with 75 Stukas plus their escorts to attack Dunkirk. It was a bad day for the Luftwaffe, as patrolling RAF fighters managed to fight through the escorts and shoot down 24 aircraft, ten of them He 111s. Bad weather intervened in favour of the Allies on 28 May and the morning of the 29th, resulting in only a handful of Luftwaffe missions over Dunkirk. By the afternoon of 29 May, the weather had cleared enough to allow 175 Luftwaffe bombers to attack. At this point, attacks with the Heinkels and Dorniers were overshadowed by 235 Stuka sorties by the VIII Fliegerkorps and Luftflotte 2. The Germans had learned a hard lesson on 27 May, so that now German bombers and Stukas were operating with larger escorts than before.

German losses were now lower, with only 16 aircraft lost that day in contrast to the 24 aircraft lost on the 27th. On 30 May, heavy clouds and rain inhibited Luftwaffe operations once more, with only a handful of German sorties in the Dunkirk area.

RAF Fighter Command No. 11 Group, which had a strength of 16 Hurricane Spitfire squadrons, began the campaign by maintaining two squadrons of British fighters over Dunkirk, with squadrons sent to cover Dunkirk at 50-minute intervals. Thus, during the long daylight hours of May and June, 11 Group fighters were typically flying three or more sorties a day over Dunkirk. The British radar system provided some assistance in guiding the RAF fighters to their station, but the limited British radar range rendered it ineffective in providing early warning of German attacks, which were normally at a strength of one or two groups, always with a group of Bf 109 or Bf 110 escorts. With only two British fighter squadrons on station at any time, the RAF would fight outnumbered by the Luftwaffe fighter escorts.

By 30 May, the British had changed tactics to allow for larger patrols of two or three squadrons, with the wing strength to cover Dunkirk and meet German fighter groups on more equal terms. This prefigured the 'big wing' concept used in the latter half of the Battle of Britain. Yet at this point in the war, RAF fighter squadrons had not yet been trained to operate in large groups with numerous fighter squadrons flying at different altitudes and positioned to support one another when contact was made. In any case, once contact was made, a general mêlé of the fighters ensued. German twin-engine bombers concentrated

Stukas of VIII Fliegerkorps bombing Calais in May 1940. The British and French garrison at Calais stood up to a German siege lasting from 22 through 26 May 1940. (AC)

Luftwaffe bombs exploding on the Dunkirk beaches. (AC)

their efforts on the Dunkirk port and the beaches while the Stukas, the most accurate bombers of 1940, concentrated on attacking Allied ships.

Aerial combat over Dunkirk between 26 May and the end of Operation *Dynamo* on 2 June was exceptionally intense. During the seven days of the campaign, British Hurricane and Spitfire squadrons lost 15 to 20 aircraft on most days. The intensity of combat with such losses, plus the damage to aircraft that returned, meant that squadrons might be down to half strength in two or three days of operations. But Fighter Command pulled decimated 11 Group squadrons out of the fight and put in full-strength squadrons from one of Fighter Command's other three groups. Thus, during the campaign for Dunkirk, 31 of Fighter Command's squadrons – that is, more than half of the total – were rotated through 11 Group so that 11 Group was able to maintain a strength of 16 squadrons with approximately 200 aircraft during the whole period of the Dunkirk evacuation. In addition, light bombers of Coastal Command carried out attacks against German forces on the perimeter, and Bomber Command sent Blenheims and medium bombers in day and night attacks against the German forces moving against the Dunkirk perimeter.

By 4 June, when the Dunkirk evacuation was completed, 338,000 British and French soldiers had been withdrawn from Dunkirk, saving the BEF and a large portion of France's best mechanized troops of the 1st and 7th Armies. Yet while Dunkirk was an Allied triumph, of sorts, in saving the personnel, virtually all the equipment of the BEF and the French First Army Group had been lost. In addition, losses in shipping had been heavy, with 124,000

Aerial view of Dunkirk's port taken 27–28 May 1940. (AC)

tons of civilian merchant shipping sunk, mostly by Luftwaffe Stukas, along with six Royal Navy and two French Navy destroyers.

In Fighter Command's first great air battle with the Luftwaffe, Spitfire and Hurricane pilots claimed more than 300 German aircraft shot down. The Air Ministry estimated that the Germans lost 390 aircraft, and Air Marshal Keith Park, 11 Group Commander, estimated that his fighters had shot down and destroyed at least 258 German aircraft, with another 119 either destroyed or severely damaged, for a total of 377 aircraft. The Royal Navy's anti-aircraft crews operating at Dunkirk claimed a further 35 German aircraft. In fact, all these pilot claims were grossly exaggerated, with the usual

The Citadel of Boulogne, shattered by 1,000lb, delayed-fuse bombs. After the Polish campaign, the Luftwaffe expressed a need for bombs that could penetrate and destroy fortifications. So, during the seven months of the Phoney War, the Luftwaffe designed and produced a new armour-piercing, 1,000lb bomb with a delayed-impact fuse that allowed the bomb to penetrate deep through concrete or masonry fortifications and then explode deep within them, thus increasing the blast effect. VIII Fliegerkorps Stukas used these bombs to shatter defences at Calais and Boulogne in May 1940. (AC)

problem of two or three fighter planes claiming the same kill, or reporting any aircraft diving away from the action or showing smoke from engine exhaust as a shoot-down. Actually, for the entire period of the air battle, the Luftwaffe lost a total of 132 aircraft across the entire French-Belgian front. Of these, approximately 100 aircraft, including 45 twin-engine bombers and ten Stukas, were lost over the Dunkirk sector. RAF Fighter Command lost 106 Spitfires and Hurricanes over Dunkirk, with likely more losses as some severely damaged aircraft were written off the records days after the battle.

Preparing for *Fall Rot*

As soon as the German forces reached the Channel on 20 May and completed the envelopment of the Allied northern armies, the German High Command and the Luftwaffe began planning for the final phase of the campaign. This would be a massive offensive by the Germans along the line of the Somme to the Aisne rivers, with the objective of taking Paris and advancing deep into France, forcing a French surrender.

Even as the Allied forces were being forced into the Dunkirk pocket, the German Army and Luftwaffe were being reorganized for the final offensive. By 28 May, orders were issued to the two German Army groups and to Luftflotten 2 and 3 for the *Fall Rot* offensive scheduled to begin on 5 June. General von Bock's Army Group B would consist of 44 divisions placed on the German right flank and would make use of the three bridgeheads across the Somme the Germans had captured to penetrate the French left flank with an armoured thrust, advance to the Seine, and destroy the French 3rd Army Group holding the left flank. On the eastern flank, Generaloberst von Rundstedt's Army Group A, with 45 divisions, would advance from the Aisne River to Reims to destroy the French Second Army Group holding the French right flank. The two German drives would envelop Paris, and Army Group A would also advance south and cut off the 17 divisions of the French Army Group holding the Maginot Line, which were held in place by German Army Group C positioned on the German/French border.

The German High Command's directive of 24 May outlined the Luftwaffe's role in *Fall Rot*, which was to maintain air superiority by relentlessly attacking the French airfields, provide direct support especially to the Panzer units and in the breakthrough battles, and to attack targets in the French rear to restrict the movement of French reinforcements. This

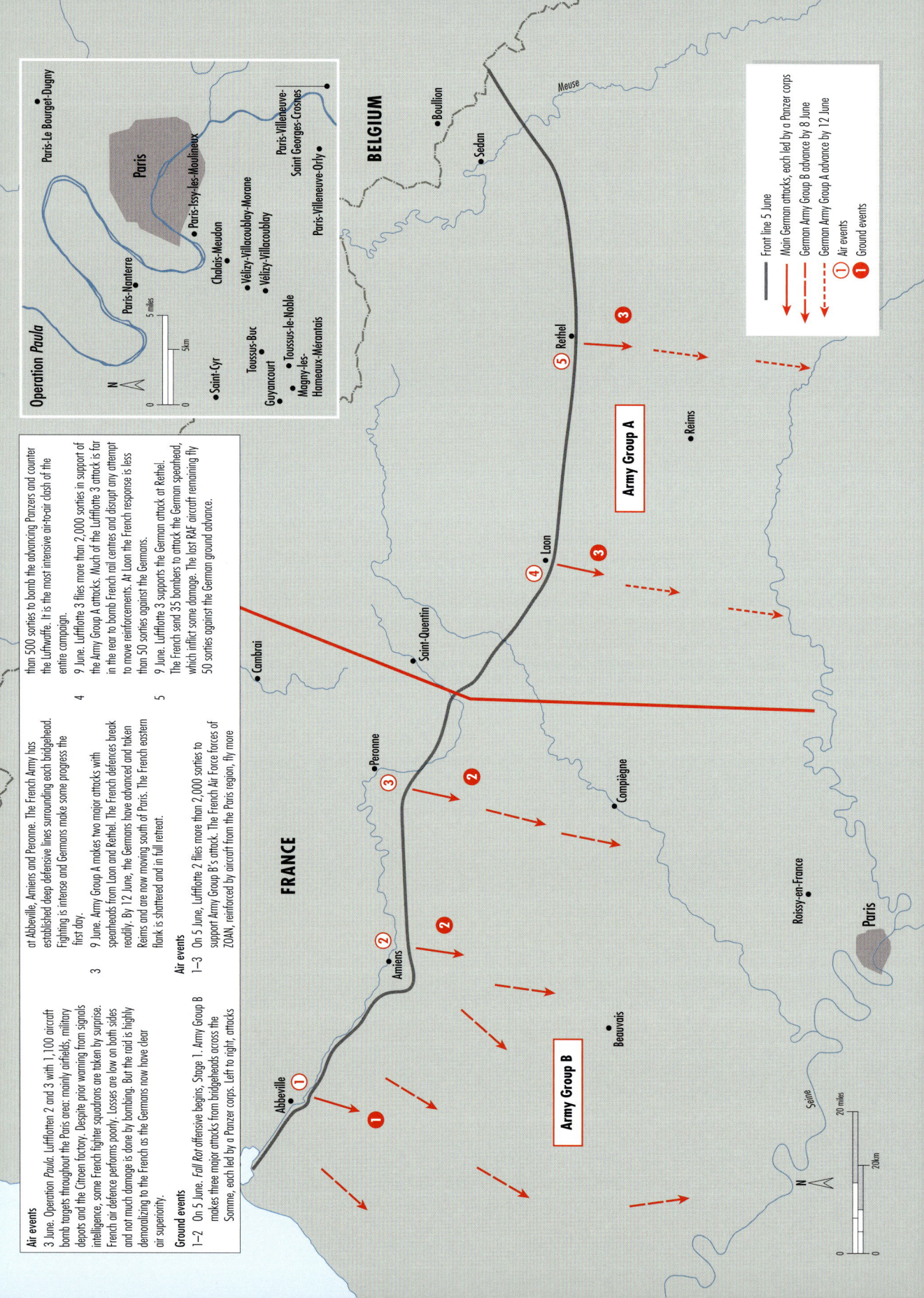

Operation Paula

(inset map, Paris area)

Paris-Le Bourget-Dugny
Paris
Paris-Nanterre
Paris-Issy-les-Moulineux
Chalais-Meudon
Vélizy-Villacoublay-Morane
Vélizy-Villacoublay
Paris-Villeneuve-Saint Georges-Croches
Paris-Villeneuve-Orly
Saint-Cyr
Toussus-Buc
Guyancourt
Toussus-le-Noble
Magny-les-Hameaux-Mérantais

5 miles
5km

Air events

3 June. Operation *Paula*. Luftflotten 2 and 3 with 1,100 aircraft bomb targets throughout the Paris area: mainly airfields, military depots and the Citroen factory. Despite prior warning from signals intelligence, some French fighter squadrons are taken by surprise. French air defence performs poorly. Losses are low on both sides and not much damage is done by bombing. But the raid is highly demoralizing to the French as the Germans now have clear air superiority.

Ground events

1–2 On 5 June, *Fall Rot* offensive begins, Stage 1. Army Group B makes three major attacks from bridgeheads across the Somme, each led by a Panzer corps. Left to right, attacks at Abbeville, Amiens and Peronne. The French Army has established deep defensive lines surrounding each bridgehead. Fighting is intense and Germans make some progress the first day.

3 9 June. Army Group A makes two major attacks with spearheads from Laon and Rethel. The French defences break readily. By 12 June, the Germans have advanced and taken Reims and are now moving south of Paris. The French eastern flank is shattered and in full retreat.

Air events

1–3 On 5 June, Luftflotte 2 flies more than 2,000 sorties to support Army Group B's attack. The French Air Force forces of ZOAN, reinforced by aircraft from the Paris region, fly more than 500 sorties to bomb the advancing Panzers and counter the Luftwaffe. It is the most intensive air-to-air clash of the entire campaign.

4 9 June. Luftflotte 3 flies more than 2,000 sorties in support of the Army Group A attacks. Much of the Luftflotte 3 attack is far in the rear to bomb French rail centres and disrupt any attempt to move reinforcements. At Laon the French response is less than 50 sorties against the Germans.

5 9 June. Luftflotte 3 supports the German attack at Rethel. The French send 35 bombers to attack the German spearhead, which inflict some damage. The last RAF aircraft remaining fly 50 sorties against the German ground advance.

Legend

— Front line 5 June
→ Main German attacks, each led by a Panzer corps
→ German Army Group B advance by 8 June
⇢ German Army Group A advance by 12 June
(1) Air events
1 Ground events

BELGIUM
FRANCE

Meuse
Boullion
Sedan
Rethel
Reims
Saint-Quentin
Cambrai
Laon
Peronne
Compiègne
Amiens
Beauvais
Abbeville
Roissy-en-France
Paris
Seine

Army Group A
Army Group B

20 miles
20km

OPPOSITE FINAL PHASE OF CAMPAIGN: *FALL ROT*

meant attacking rail lines and junctions deep into France. The Luftwaffe was also to spot and ruthlessly target any French attempts to regroup their forces.

Luftflotten 2 and 3 were to be reorganized to support their mission. Most of the bomber groups would be concentrated in Luftflotte 2, as their mission on the German right flank would include long-range attacks against the French Atlantic Coast ports. Most of the Stuka units were transferred to Luftflotte 3, whose task it was to break the centre of the French lines and whose Panzer forces would likely require more direct support. Thus, as the Dunkirk campaign was concluding, the Luftwaffe on the Western Front was reorganized for the final phase of the Battle of France. Luftflotte 2 would command 21 Kampfgruppen, eight Jagdgruppen, two Zerstörergruppen, one Stuka group, and six reconnaissance squadrons, which would also retain 2 Flakkorps. Luftflotte 3 would command 14 Jagdgruppen and seven Zerstörergruppen, 15 Kampfgruppen, and nine Stuka/Schlachtgruppen. Both air fleets would have six Dornier 17 long-range reconnaissance squadrons. The total Luftwaffe force for the final battle would consist of 1,000 aircraft for Luftflotte 2, and 1,500 aircraft for Luftflotte 3.

Due to heavy fighting and losses in the May battles, the Luftwaffe air fleets had fewer aircraft than at the start of the campaign, but considering the state of the French Air Force, the Germans would still enjoy a better than 2:1 advantage against the French. The Luftwaffe redeployed one Bf 109 group to the North Sea coast of the Netherlands, and the Luftwaffe pulled four medium bomber groups out of the battle to be sent to Germany and reequipped with Ju 88s. The Luftwaffe losses for the first phase of the campaign had been heavy. Approximately a third of the Luftwaffe's aircraft in the west had been lost or severely damaged in combat since 10 May. However, the Luftwaffe took action to ensure that most aircraft and aircrew losses could be quickly replaced.

Generaloberst Erhard Milch, the State Secretary for Aviation, worked to speed up the flow of replacement aircraft to front units during the campaign. He directed the Luftwaffe training schools to send course graduates from the Fighter, Bomber, Stuka, and Reconnaissance schools directly to the front-line Luftwaffe units instead of the usual procedure of assigning new personnel to training squadrons for several weeks before rotating them into combat.

Bf 109s demonstrating a four-ship formation, standard for Luftwaffe fighters. On a combat patrol, there would usually be 150m between aircraft, thus allowing a flight of four to effectively cover a large area. (AC)

Another directive issued by Milch ordered some instructor pilots and aircrew from the advanced flight schools to be sent as replacements to Luftflotten 2 and 3. Thus, by the start of the final offensive on 5 June, most of the Luftwaffe units now had most of their aircrew and aircraft on hand. There were pilot and aircrew shortages, and Von Richthofen's VIII Fliegerkorps Stuka groups had not seen all their losses replaced. But Milch's efforts ensured that the tired Luftwaffe bomber, Stuka, and fighter groups were reasonably ready to begin the final battle for France.

In preparation for *Fall Rot*, Luftflotte 3 sent bomber formations

deep into France, bombing targets in the Rhône valley and targeting southern French cities. These attacks again highlighted the vulnerability of French cities and increased pressure on the French Air Force to maintain fighters in the rear to protect French industries.

In preparation for *Fall Rot*, the German Army reorganized its Panzer and motorized forces into five groups. Three would act as the spearheads for Army Group B's bridgeheads over the Somme, and two Panzer groups would spearhead Army Group A's advance from the Aisne. As with the offensive at Sedan, the Luftwaffe's motorized flak regiments of Flakkorps I and II would be divided among the Panzer-led attack columns. Once the breakthroughs were made by the Panzer and motorized forces, then all the German infantry corps were to advance along the attack length of France's northern front. Both army groups were to position themselves to encircle Paris from both east and west, while maintaining a rapid advance along other sectors of the front.

French preparations for the final phase

The German attack on 10 May had come in the middle of a programme to reequip l'Armée de l'Air with a series of modern aircraft. Though French aircraft production had steadily increased from the start of the war, by May 1940 production rates were still little more than half of the 750 aircraft per month that the French Air Ministry had projected in its production schedules. Still, the French Air Force was now receiving enough modern aircraft to not only replace losses, but also to reequip fighter and bomber units with both French LeO and Potez light bombers and American Martin and Douglas bombers. In fighter groups, obsolescent Morane-Saulnier M.S.406s were replaced with superior Curtiss Hawks, and enough Dewoitine D.520 fighters – the one aircraft in the French inventory that could match the Bf 109 – were arriving to reequip several groups.

Even after the heavy losses taken by the French Air Force in May, in terms of aircraft numbers the French Air Force was paradoxically improving. By early June, the French industry purchases had been delivered: 599 modern fighters, 309 bombers, and 116 reconnaissance airplanes, a total of 1,024 aircraft. On paper, that actually increased the French Air Force to over 2,000 aircraft. However, of the 2,086 combat aircraft on the French Air Force books

An RAF Hawker Hurricane Mk. I. The Hawker Hurricane was the RAF's primary fighter plane in 1939–40 and formed the fighter element of the RAF in France. Though powered by a 1,030hp Rolls-Royce Merlin engine, the Hurricane was slower than its Bf 109 opponents or the RAF's Spitfire. However, it was highly manoeuvrable and could outmanoeuvre a Bf 109 at lower altitudes. While the Spitfire was superior in most respects, the Hurricane with its thicker wing made a better gun platform for its eight .303 machine guns. The Hurricanes rendered good service in the 1940 campaign over France and in the Battle of Britain. Later, adapted with cannon, the Hurricane made an excellent fighter bomber. (AC)

on 1 June, only 600 were fully operational; 1,087 were either unserviceable from minor damage, or more commonly, were sitting in air depots awaiting modifications or installation of armament, radios, and instruments. The situation for bombers was especially dire, as many of the excellent Martin and Douglas bombers imported from America were flyable, but were sitting on rear airfields for weeks and even months while awaiting necessary equipment such as bombsights, bomb-release gear, radios, and machine guns.

France's new Commander-in-Chief General Maxime Weygand took command on 19 May as the hapless General Gamelin was relieved. Weygand strongly supported using French bombers in close support of the ground battle. After the Germans reached the Channel on 20 May, d'Astier further reorganized his own forces to create assault forces. The primary concern of the French were the three bridgeheads that Von Kleist's Panzergruppe had established across the Somme, as these were the most obvious routes for the German invasion of the rest of France, which was expected to come soon. While Von Kleist's divisions were being reorganized and resupplied, the German bridgeheads were garrisoned by infantry corps. The newly created French Tenth Army, which faced the German bridgehead at Abbeville, planned the major offensive to crush the German bridgehead on 4 June. Prior to the attack, d'Astier had created a provisional assault air brigade consisting of 43 Breguet bombers, supported by 40 fighters, and he offered this force to support General Altmayer, the Tenth Army commander. D'Astier told the Tenth Army that he had 50 more bombers and 100 more fighters available for general air support to attack the Somme bridgeheads. To this offer, Altmayer replied, 'What am I to do with all this aviation? I've already got more than sufficient artillery.' The Tenth Army carried out its offensive and pushed back the bridgeheads, but failed to eliminate them, having declined the support of nearly 250 aircraft.

In anticipation of a final German offensive, Vuillemin reorganized his front air forces, creating a new air force command in the centre that would operate subordinate to ZOAN. ZOAE was reinforced, and an RAF force consisting of three Hurricane squadrons and a wing

Luftwaffe's top fighter pilot shot down by French D.520

In June 1940, Hauptmann Werner Mölders was famous as Germany's top fighter pilot. Commanding a Condor Legion squadron of Bf 109 fighters in Spain in 1938, Mölders discarded the tight formations and fighter tactics of World War I and developed loose fighter formations and tactics based on pairs of fighters supporting each other. These tactics gave Luftwaffe fighters a big advantage over their opponents. In Spain, Mölders shot down 14 aircraft and in May–June 1940 he added another 15 victories to his tally.

In 1940, Mölders commanded III Group of Jagdgeschwader 53, equipped with the Bf 109E fighter. At 1840hrs on 5 June, one of the most intensive days of aerial combat in the whole campaign, Mölders led a patrol of 18 JG 53 fighters when they encountered a patrol of eight Dewoitine D.520 French fighters from CG II/7 just south of Beauvais. The D.520s, equal to the Bf 109 in speed, manoeuvrability, and armament (one 20mm cannon and four 7.5mm machine guns), had just been introduced to the French Air Force, and the Germans mistook the D.520s for the slower and less manoeuvrable Morane-Saulnier M.S.406 fighters. It was an almost fatal mistake for Mölders.

The fight dropped to 2,400ft and a series of combats began. Mölders was spotted by French pilot Lieutenant René Pomier Layrargues, who had earned his pilot wings in 1937 and had distinguished himself by shooting down four German bombers in May. Layrargues turned his plane towards Mölders and fired and missed. Mölders and Layrargues then banked in opposite directions. Mölders, thinking he was fighting a M.S.406, lost sight of his opponent and assumed he had dropped out of the fight. But Layrargues, using the speed and manoeuvrability of his D.520, had whipped his aircraft into a tight turn that put him just behind and below Mölders. Layrargues put a burst of fire into Mölder's engine. Having only seconds before his plane went out of control, Mölders detached his canopy and threw himself out of his Bf 109. He was quickly captured by French soldiers and became a POW for two weeks until the armistice between France and Germany required the return of France's German POWs.

Layrargues did not have time to celebrate his becoming an ace as he was shot down and killed in another engagement 30 minutes after his victory. Captain Mölders went on to command Jagdgeschwader 51 during the Battle of Britain and in Russia. In July 1941, he became the first fighter pilot of World War II to claim 100 aerial victories. He was promoted to colonel and made the Luftwaffe's Inspector of Fighters. He was killed as a passenger in an aircraft accident in November 1941.

of Blenheim bombers remained in France to support the eastern flank, where the Germans were expected to mount a major offensive across the Aisne River. The main French effort would remain with ZOAN on the western flank, as the German bridgeheads on the Somme were considered the greatest threat. D'Astier, who previously could count on some fighter support coming from the large fighter force protecting Paris, could now fully draw upon the fighters around the capital, which were now within range of the German lines.

Concerned by their shortage of fighters compared to the Germans, the French government requested that the RAF Fighter Command send a large part of its forces to help defend France in this final battle, but the British declined. This led to some bitterness on the part of the French, who thought that the British had abandoned them at their most dangerous moment. Yet the RAF was behaving exactly like the French Air Force, which had a considerable number of fighters, at least 200, far in the rear protecting French cities, aircraft factories, and Marseille. Neither the French nor the British governments could afford the outcry if their populations were left unprotected from German bombers.

Operation *Paula*: the Luftwaffe bombs Paris

The Germans had long planned for a massive air attack in the Paris region as a prelude to a massive ground invasion. Attacking a large number of targets in and around Paris, the Germans thought, would be a massive blow to French morale and provide a demonstration of the Luftwaffe's air superiority. At midday on 3 June, Luftflotten 2 and 3 launched 640 bombers escorted by 460 fighters to attack 16 French airfields and depots around Paris, with a further dozen French aircraft and arms factories also targeted.

The French ought to have been ready for the Luftwaffe attack because British cryptographers had intercepted and decoded some of the Luftwaffe's operational plans, sent using their Enigma machines in a code that the British had recently broken. However, the Germans had their own electronic warfare method. The French Air Force used the radio transmitter atop the Eiffel Tower to broadcast signals to all the French squadrons in central France and on 3 June the Luftwaffe jammed the French transmission. Thus, some French squadrons

German airmen receiving a group mission briefing before taking off. All the German squadron and group commanders and staffs had been thoroughly trained at the Luftwaffe's Luftkreisschule in planning and executing tactical missions. (AC)

RAF radio operators at a wing headquarters in France in spring 1940. The RAF possessed a better communications infrastructure than l'Armée de l'Air during the 1940 campaign. (IWM)

received no warning of the German attack, and they would have to take off and climb to attack under German bombing. Other French squadrons received warnings that were received late, and two Bloch MB. 152 groups took off but were intercepted as they climbed by Bf 109 escorts, and eight were shot down.

German bombers attacking Paris reported only sporadic anti-aircraft fire. Bombers attacking from 10,000ft were out of range of light anti-aircraft guns, while the heavier 75mm anti-aircraft guns were mostly obsolete and not very accurate. The German attackers noted that the French heavy anti-aircraft guns that did come into action appeared to fire without proper control.

In the attack on Paris, the Luftwaffe's attacking force lost only four bombers as the escort fighters managed to successfully engage the French fighters before they reached the bombers. For its part, the French fighter force gave a good showing in air-to-air combat with Bf 109s, the French losing 16 fighters to the Luftwaffe's losses of 14 fighters. As for damage, the large raid from 10,000ft was not very accurate and inflicted only slight to moderate damage on the French airfields. While the Germans claimed hundreds of French aircraft destroyed on the ground, in reality only a couple of dozen French aircraft were destroyed or heavily damaged. The French factories attacked also received mostly light damage, though part of a Citroën truck factory was destroyed.

In actual effects, Operation *Paula* was not the powerful blow against French aviation that the Luftwaffe had hoped for. But it did prove that German bombers could attack France's most heavily defended city with relative impunity, and with minimal losses. Paris ought to have had a highly effective integrated fighter-anti-aircraft defensive system. Despite prior warning, the attack was a clear demonstration that the French Air Force had failed to create an effective air defence command in the Paris region.

Unlike Britain and Germany, which had both developed effective radar systems for homeland defence, in the 1930s France had not invested in radar research. Instead, the French aerial early warning system relied upon teams of ground aerial observers, spread thinly along the front to provide information on German aircraft formations, and their altitude and direction as the Germans crossed the front. Using a cumbersome reporting system, ground observer air reports worked their way from army units to the air force communications system. By the time French fighters in the rear got the message, the German bombers had usually already arrived at their target and dropped their bombs. The system was so ineffective that French fighter groups developed their own system for sending warning messages to all other groups in their air regions whenever an airfield was attacked.

It also highlights the failure of the French Air Force to ensure that all its aircraft had adequate radios, capable of communicating not only within a fighter group, but with other groups as well. French fighter groups were commonly unable to communicate with the other fighter or bomber groups flying on the same mission. One of the key deficiencies in the French logistics system was the lack of radios, which kept many of the new bombers and fighters on the ground.

Fall Rot: the final offensive

On 5 June, Army Group B attacked out of its bridgeheads at Abbeville, Amiens, and Péronne on the Somme. D'Astier focused his available bomber strength towards attacking the French front line. An attack by ten Breguets escorted by fighters in the early morning was carried out without losses, but in a later strike by 12 Breguets without escort, nine were shot down by Bf 109s patrolling the front. All further bomber attacks were heavily escorted by the fighters.

The timing of the German attack on the French western flank was similar to that of the German invasion of the Low Countries on 10 May – it focused the effort of the French High Command on one area. Aircraft were redeployed from other regions to meet the threat, and four fighter groups in the Paris area were ordered to support the battle on the Somme front. During 5 June, the French fighter force flew 487 sorties, the highest number of daily sorties since the campaign had begun. The aerial fighting was intense, and it was clear that the French Air Force had improved greatly since the start of the campaign. In supporting that offensive on the Somme, the Luftwaffe lost 40 aircraft, of which 22 were bombers.

Still, the maximum effort of the French Air Force amounted to a single fighter sortie a day for most of the French fighter units. On the ground side, the German attacks on all three bridgeheads had made progress, but the greatest success was at Abbeville, where the 7th Panzer Division had managed a six-mile advance.

The French had expected that their large concentration of artillery surrounding the three bridgeheads would be effective in stopping the German advance. But German aircraft flew overhead most of the day and French artillery refrained from shooting while German aircraft were overhead, knowing that the flash of their well-camouflaged guns would immediately draw German bombers and Stukas onto their positions. Thus, German air superiority over

Luftwaffe Ju 52 transport delivering fuel to a forward airfield, June 1940. The Luftwaffe's ability to maintain the flow of fuel and munitions to forward airfields was one of the keys to the Luftwaffe's success in spring 1940. (AC)

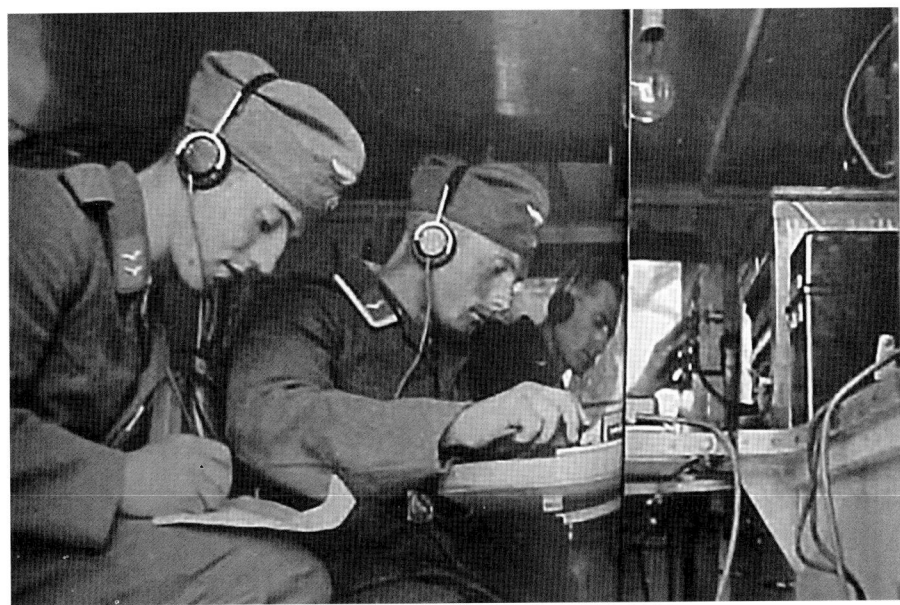

Luftwaffe signals detachment at a forward airfield. The Luftwaffe had a command-and-control system far superior to that of the Allied forces. (AC)

the battlefield worked effectively to nullify the one really effective defensive weapon that the French Army possessed.

The first stages of the final campaign beginning on 5 June saw an intense effort to pulverize the French in-depth defences around the Somme bridgeheads. It was a day of relatively heavy losses, with 40 Luftwaffe aircraft lost. However, the intensity of the German effort was reflected in the sortie rate of JG 27's 85 available aircraft. On 5 June alone, JG 27 flew 265 sorties, which was about half of what the entire French fighter force in the north flew on that day.

The German efforts to grind down the French defences were successful, with moderate gains by German Panzer forces on the first day, followed by encirclement and isolation of French strongpoints on the next two days. By the evening of 8 June, the French left flank was now wide open, with few organized forces available to stop the Germans from crossing the Seine and advancing farther south.

On 9 June, the Army Group A offensive began, with its main push being the area of Soissons and Rethel, and breaking of the French defence lines along the Aisne River, held by the French Fourth Army. On 9 June, as a preliminary bombardment, II Fliegerkorps bombers first struck the Fourth Army's reserves and rear area for two hours, and concluded with a one-hour bombardment of the Fourth Army's main defence line with 572 bomber, Stuka, and fighter sorties. Even though II Fliegerkorps' medium bombers were still based in western Germany, they still managed to fly two sorties that day. In a scene similar to that at Sedan, the French defenders could not hold up against that level of aerial pressure. By the end of the day, Army Group A's Panzers had advanced several miles, and by the 10th, it was clear that the defence on France's right flank was hopelessly lost, as the German spearhead forces made rapid advances along a broad front.

The French Air Force Eastern Zone attempted a handful of bomber sorties against the German rear, but these had little effect on the Germans while costing the French more bombers and fighters when they engaged II Fliegerkorps fighters patrolling the front. On the evening of 9 June, the French Air Force wanted to send a strong bomber force against the German breakthrough, but only 17 bombers were available.

The two German Army groups had broken through both French flanks and were now advancing deep into France, facing only sporadic organized resistance. There was no longer any hope for the French Army defending Paris, and on 10 June, the French government evacuated the capital and fled to Bordeaux. On 11 June, with German armoured forces now flanking Paris to both east and west, Paris was declared an open city. The French Army was in headlong retreat and attempted delaying actions, while the French Air Force was forced to evacuate its airfields. The French Air Force moved units based in the Paris region to airfields in central France and to training fields in southern France. The Germans quickly occupied the French airfields, only to find them filled with aircraft that had been abandoned, many of them only slightly damaged, and others unflyable due solely to a lack of parts. This was the price that France paid for having an air force logistics and repair system that was inadequate, even for peacetime operations, and which had largely collapsed due to the pressures of war.

With the breakthrough operations over, Luftflotten 2 and 3 turned to other missions. Luftflotte 2 turned from attacking French airfields (between 5 and 9 June, 19 French airfields came under their heavy attack) and now focused on attacking French Atlantic ports and shipping, beginning on 9 June. Cherbourg, Le Havre, Saint-Nazaire, and Bordeaux were bombed both by day and night for the remainder of the campaign. The greatest single Allied shipping loss came on 17 June when the British liner *Lancastria*, evacuating both military personnel and civilians from France, was sunk by German bombers, with 5,800 lives lost. However, despite the attacks, the British managed to evacuate 192,000 Allied personnel through the French ports before the armistice went into effect. Evacuees included the remnants, service, and support personnel of the BEF, still stationed in France, plus the ground crews of the RAF remaining in France. Many thousands of Polish soldiers and airmen who had been training with the French as well as many Czech pilots were among the evacuees.

While the Germans now had an abundance of aircraft, few were needed for close support of ground operations. For the first time since the campaign had begun on 10 May, Von Richthofen was able to order that half of his Stuka aircrew were to be given a three-day rest period, rotating with the next half. No longer did the Stukas need to fly three sorties a day.

In the meantime, while Luftflotte 2 bombers concentrated on the French Atlantic ports, Luftflotte 3's bombers concentrated on paralyzing the rail network of eastern and central France by staging large attacks on key rail centres. The campaign against French rail was fairly effective, and any chance that the French could create a general reserve or quickly mass forces for a counterattack was eliminated.

After the decisive German breakthroughs and the German occupation of Paris on 14 June, the main activity of the French Air Force was using its fighters to attack the German bombers, but with little success as the German bombers were well escorted. With no chance of victory in Metropolitan France, Vuillemin ordered the most modern aircraft of the Air Force to be evacuated to North Africa, which would enable France to fight on, if necessary, but would also save France's best aircraft from being captured by the Germans. Between 15 and 22 June, the French Air Force managed to fly between 700–800 of their aircraft to safety in North Africa. This included all the flyable Martin, Douglas, LeO, and Breguet bombers as well as the Dewoitine D.520 fighters. Now that the French air industry was producing significant numbers of modern aircraft, many of the rescued aircraft were flown straight from the factory to North Africa.

The greatest impediment to German air operations in the breakthrough was the bad weather from 10–13 June, which reduced German flights to a minimum. After the weather cleared, the attacks on French ports, airfields, and rail stations continued. There remained few lucrative targets for the German bomber groups, so by the 17th, Luftflotte 3/KG 2 was flying supply-drop missions to replenish the fuel of Panzer division spearheads that were now so deep into central France that they had outrun their supply lines. On 18 June, the new French government, now headed by Marshal Philippe Pétain, initiated discussions with the Germans to negotiate an armistice. On 19 June, the German air campaign effectively ended. Negotiations began and on 22 June, the French and German governments agreed to an armistice that took France out of the war.

OPPOSITE
French soldiers man a 75mm anti-aircraft gun, April 1940. A large proportion of the French flak forces were equipped with obsolete World War I anti-aircraft guns. (AC)

ANALYSIS AND CONCLUSION

The campaign for France in 1940 was fought by the Germans as a truly modern joint warfare operation with close coordination of air and ground forces working together to fulfill the operational and strategic objectives. The joint approach became a model for the Allied Powers, who developed their own models, organization, and doctrine that became the norm for the British and American air and ground forces.

A French 25mm Hotchkiss light anti-aircraft gun. This was an excellent gun that equalled the performance of German light flak, but France had only 500 of these guns in 1940 versus thousands of German light flak guns. (AC)

Leadership

The British and French forces in 1940 failed mainly because of poor military leadership at the top. Allied Supreme Commander General Maurice Gamelin had a 1918 understanding of warfare and saw air forces as only a secondary support force for the ground army. He rarely consulted with the senior air commanders and saw little use for employing bombers in the ground campaign. French Air Force Chief of Staff General Vuillemin was noted for his inaction. He took command of an air force in early 1938 suffering from severe personnel problems, poor organization, and a dysfunctional logistics system. He failed to take any action to deal with these problems that could have been solved by the start of the battle. RAF chief, Air Chief Marshal Newell, was an excellent administrator and manager of the RAF before the war, but his devotion to the strategic bomber theory kept him from using Bomber Command in the ground battle when it could have had a major impact.

The top German airmen were all intelligent and pragmatic. State Secretary for Aviation Generaloberst Milch had overseen the build-up of the Luftwaffe and ensured it had an excellent mobile logistics and support infrastructure. Under his tenure, the Luftwaffe was the only major air force of the time that had a large contingent of transport aircraft, a key factor to the success of the Wehrmacht in 1940. Air Fleet commanders Sperrle and Kesselring had already successfully commanded large air forces in major campaigns where air support for the ground armies was a main focus of operations. Air Corps Commander Generalmajor von Richthofen can be singled out as the top expert of any air force of the time in the art of providing air support to ground armies.

The subordinate Allied air commanders, RAF Air Marshal Barratt, and Air Vice Marshal Playfair, made practical attempts to change their doctrine and tactics before the battle but were stymied by their superiors. French General d'Astier, who worked well with his British counterparts and tried providing air support to the ground forces, had to deal with French Army generals who had no understanding of how to plan and operate with air forces.

Command and control

In terms of using airpower, the Allied command and control was fragmented, as the RAF commanders in France had to request bomber support from the Air Staff in London. The French had divided their control at the front between army-controlled air units and those of the sector commander. The French system of dividing the air forces into zone command was fine for peacetime administration, but not in combat. The German system of air fleets corresponding to army groups, and air corps corresponding to ground armies – and all with organic logistics and support organizations – made for rapid and effective responses to all the situations that arose during the battle.

Doctrine and training

Allied air doctrine had ignored the employment of airpower in coordination with the ground forces at the operational level during the interwar period. The French and British air forces had all been too enamoured with the promise of decisive air victory through strategic bombing campaigns and lacked effective means to coordinate air and ground forces, although Air Marshal Barratt and General d'Astier had worked to improve army/air liaison and coordination. However, it is difficult, if not impossible, to introduce new doctrines in the middle of a campaign.

The Germans had a very sound doctrine for a multi-purpose air force since the founding of the Luftwaffe. Since 1935, the Luftwaffe had conducted regular large- and small-scale manoeuvres alongside their army counterparts. Luftwaffe officer training had emphasized joint operations. The Luftwaffe had an excellent system of air liaison officers (FLIVOs) with good communications to ensure that the air commanders were well informed of ground operations and could respond quickly to crises. The Luftwaffe was the only air force in the world that could respond to calls for air support in 45–75 minutes. The campaigns in Spain and Poland had proved that aircraft used as flying artillery could break through well-defended enemy positions.

Training armies and air forces to operate effectively together takes years. In 1940, the Allies lacked the training and experience of the Germans. Not one of the major Allied counterattacks in May and June 1940 was provided with adequate air support – although there were plenty of bombers and fighters that could have been deployed. In contrast, every Allied counterattack was met with a strong and immediate response by the Luftwaffe, which helped ensure that all the Allied counterattacks failed. All the major German attacks were very effectively supported by the Luftwaffe. Indeed, the Luftwaffe receives equal credit for the brilliant success of German arms in 1940 with the Panzer divisions.

Tactics

The British and French air forces had serious deficiencies at the tactical level of war in 1940. Neither Britain nor France had put much emphasis on the anti-aircraft arm, which was a sideline of the artillery branch in the French and British armies. In Germany, the Luftwaffe

controlled the flak arm and built a large mobile force to defend Germany and cooperate with the army. In 1940, the British and French combined had far fewer anti-aircraft guns than the Germans, and most of the heavy anti-aircraft guns were obsolete guns from the last world war. On the northern front, where most combat action took place, the Luftwaffe had approximately 1,500 modern heavy and light flak guns, while the Allies had no more than 800. Moreover, German doctrine encouraged the use of flak guns in direct support of the ground troops, where the 88, 37, and 20mm rapid-fire cannons were highly effective destroying enemy fortifications and tanks. To the rear, the Germans had enough guns to provide strong flak defences to defend key points and free up the fighters from standing patrols which allowed for large escorts for Luftwaffe bombers. Luftwaffe flak efficiently decimated Allied air attacks at Maastricht, the Sedan bridges, and at Berliamont.

The Germans had developed tactics in Spain and Poland on how to use Stukas and bombers to best effect. Stukas routinely bombed from 10,000ft, which minimized the time the dive bombers would be flying low and slow and were vulnerable to ground fire. German bombers usually bombed from 10,000–15,000ft, out of range of most anti-aircraft fire. Bombing from that altitude was not very accurate in 1940, but the Luftwaffe made up for it by using at least one group (30 bombers) dropping 60+ tons of bombs per target. In contrast, the British and French normally made small squadron-strength attacks which required them to go low to try to hit the target with their small bombloads.

The British and French air forces in 1940 still used the very tight and complex fighter formations of World War I, when none of the fighters had radios and aircraft had to fly very close to see visual signals from their squadron and flight commanders. Fighter pilots spent more time looking to maintain formation and avoid collisions than they did looking for the enemy. Changing direction and formations might require a couple of minutes in battle when seconds counted. As a Bf 109 squadron commander in Spain in 1938, Hauptmann Werner Mölders developed modern tactics that were made standard by the Luftwaffe in 1938–39. As fighters now had radios and could easily communicate with each other, there was no need for close formations. Mölders directed his pilots to fly in pairs (*Rotten*) with planes 100–150m apart and the pilots covering each other. Two pairs would form a flight of four (*Schwarm*) led by a flight commander. The Schwarm would spread out as two pairs looking like an extended four fingers across half a mile of sky, which covered much more of the sky and allowed the flights to turn 90 degrees in seconds simply by switching places. Tactics consisted of loose formations of two to four aircraft, which enabled squadrons and groups to easily change formation and direction. These basic tactics were so effective in battle that the Allies would adopt them, and they are still in use today.

The campaign of 1940 was the real beginning of modern joint warfare, with armies and air forces working closely as a team. The German Army and Luftwaffe were successful in 1940 because they had spent years in developing doctrine, evolving effective command and control systems, and in training officers and whole formations to cooperate closely. The British and French in 1940 made attempts to conduct joint warfare, but such things cannot be done in the middle of a campaign. It would take the British two years of effort and in 1942, with the Desert Air Force in North Africa, the RAF and British Army could finally operate at the level the Germans had done in 1940. The British and American air forces would copy the German methods of organization, planning, command and control, plus the tactics from 1940 and by 1943–44 would develop them into the main tool for victory against Germany.

British artillerymen man a Bofors 40mm anti-aircraft gun in France. This was one of the best light anti-aircraft guns of World War II, used by many powers, but in 1940 Britain had only a few of these guns available. (Alamy))

BIBLIOGRAPHY

Alexander, Martin S., *The Republic in Danger: General Maurice Gamelin and the Politics of French Defence, 1933–1940*, Cambridge University Press, Cambridge (2003)

d'Astier de La Vigerie, François Pierre Raoul, *Le Ciel N'était Pas Vide, 1940*, Julliard, Paris (1952)

Balke, Ulf., *Der Luftkrieg in Europa 1939–1941*, Bernard und Graefe Verlag, Bonn (1990)

Baughen, G., *The RAF in the Battle of France and the Battle of Britain: A Reappraisal of Army and Air Policy 1938–1940*, Fonthill Media, Stroud (2016)

Baughen, G., *The Fairey Battle: A Reassessment of its RAF Career*, Fonthill Media, Stroud (2017)

Baughen, G., *The Rise and Fall of the French Air Force: French Air Operations and Strategy 1900–1940*, Fonthill Media, Stroud (2018)

Boog, Horst, *Die Deutsche Luftwaffenführung 1935–1945*, Deutsche Verlags-Anstalt, Stuttgart (1982)

Boog, Horst, 'Higher Command and Leadership in the German Luftwaffe, 1935–1945', *Airpower and Warfare*, ed. Alfred Hurley, 128–58, USAF Office of History, Washington, D.C. (1979)

Brown, Eric, *Wings of the Luftwaffe*, Presidio Press, Novato (1987)

Buffotot, P., 'La Perception du Réarmament Allemand Par Les Organismes Renseignements Francais de 1936 à 1939', *Revue Historique des Armeés* 3 (1979), pp. 173–84

Burdick, Charles, 'Die Deutschen Militärischen Planungen Gegenüber Frankreich, 1933–1938', *Wehrwissenschaftliche Rundschau* 6, 12 (1956), pp. 678–81

Cain, Anthony, *The Forgotten Air Force: French Air Doctrine in the 1930s*, Smithsonian History of Aviation and Spaceflight Series (2002)

Christienne, Charles, and Pierre Lissarrague, *A History of French Military Aviation*, Smithsonian Institution Press, Washington, D.C. (1986)

Cornwell, P. D., Ramsay, W. G. (ed.), *The Battle of France Then and Now: Six Nations Locked in Aerial Combat, September 1939 to June 1940*, Battle of Britain International, Old Harlow (2007)

Corum, James, 'From Biplanes to Blitzkrieg: The Development of German Air Doctrine Between the Wars', *War in History*, Vol. 3, No. 1 (1996), pp. 85–101

Corum, James, 'The Spanish Civil War: Lessons Learned and Not Learned by the Major Powers', *Journal of Military History* (1998)

Corum, James, 'Stärken und Schwächen der Luftwaffe Führungsqualitäten und Führung im Zweiten Weltkrieg' in *Die Wehrmacht: Mythos und Realität*, ed. Rolf-Dieter Mueller, Militärgeschichtliches Forschungsamt, Potsdam (1998)

Corum, James, 'The Luftwaffe's Army Support Doctrine, 1918–1941', *Journal of Military History*, (1995), pp. 53–76.

Corum, James, *The Luftwaffe: Creating the Operational Air War, 1918–1940*, University Press of Kansas, Lawrence (1997)

Corum, James, *Wolfram von Richthofen: Master of the German Air War*, University Press of Kansas, Lawrence (2008)

Corum, James and Richard R. Muller, *The Luftwaffe's Way of War: German Air Doctrine 1911–1945*, Nautical and Aviation, Baltimore (1998)

Cull, Brian, with Bruce Lander and Heinrich Weiss, *Twelve Days in May*, Grub Street, London (1999)

Cuny, Jean and Raymond Danel, *Aviation de Chasse Française, 1918–1940*, Docavia, Paris (1974)

Deichmann, Paul, *German Air Force Operations in Support of the Army*, USAF Historical Study 163, Air University Press, Maxwell Air Force Base, Alabama (1962)

Deist, Wilhelm et. al., *The Build-up of German Aggression: Germany and the Second World War*, Vol. 1, Clarendon Press, Oxford (1990)

Dierich, Wolfgang, *Kampfgeschwader 55 'Greif'*, Motorbuch Verlag, Stuttgart (1994)

Dierich, Wolfgang, *Kampfgeschwader 51 'Edelweiss'*, Motorbuch Verlag, Stuttgart (1991)

Dildy, Douglas, *Fall Gelb 1940 (1): Panzer Breakthrough in the West*, Osprey, Oxford (2014)

Doughty, Robert A., *The Breaking Point: Sedan and the Fall of France, 1940*, Stackpole Books, Mechanicsburg (2014)

Doughty, Robert, *The Seeds of Disaster: The Development of French Army Doctrine, 1919–1939*, Stackpole Books, Mechanicsburg (1986)

Dressel, Joachim and Manfred Greihl, *Bombers of the Luftwaffe*, Arms and Armour Press, London (1994)

Ellis, L. F. Butler, J. R. M. (ed.), *The War in France and Flanders 1939–1940: History of the Second World War: United Kingdom Military Series*, repr. Naval and Military Press, Uckfield ed., HMSO, London (2004) [1953]

Facon, Patrick, *L'Armée de L'Air Dans la Tourmente*, Economica, Paris (1997)

Forget, Michel, 'Die Zusammenarbeit Zwischen Luftwaffe und Heer Bei Den Französischen und Deutschen Luftstreitkräfte im Zweiten Weltkrieg', *Luftkriegführung im Zweiten Weltkrieg*, ed. Horst Boog, pp. 479–526, E. S. Mittler Verlag, Herford (1993)

Franks, Norman, *Air Battle Dunkirk, 26 May–3 June 1940*, Grub Street, London (2000)

Frieser, Karl-Heinz, *Blitzkrieg-Legende: Der Westfeldzug 1940*, Oldenbourg Verlag, Munich (1995)

Galland, Adolf, *The First and the Last*, Important Books, London (1955)

Green, William, *Warplanes of the Third Reich*, Galahad Books, New York (1970)

Griffin, David, 'The Battle of France 1940', *Aerospace Historian* (1974), pp. 144–53

Gunsberg, Jeffrey, *Divided and Conquered: The French High Command and the Defeat of the West, 1940*, Greenwood Press, Connecticut (1985)

Hastings, Max, *Bomber Command*, Simon and Schuster, New York (1989)

Hebrand, J., *Vingt-cinque Anneés de l'Aviation Militaire*, Vol. 1, Alvin Michel, Paris (1946)

Higham, Robin, *Bases of Air Strategy: Building Airfields for the RAF 1914–1945*, Airlife, Shrewsbury (1998)

Higham, Robin, (ed.), *Why Air Forces Fail: The Anatomy of Defeat*, The University Press of Kentucky, Lexington (2008)

Holmes, Tony, *Hurricane I vs Bf 110: 1940*, Osprey, Oxford (2010)

Homze, Edward L., *Arming the Luftwaffe: The Reich Air Ministry and the German Aircraft Industry, 1919–1939*, University of Nebraska Press, Lincoln 1976.

Homze, Edward L., 'The Continental Experience', *Air Power and Warfare*, eds. Alfred Hurley and Robert Ehrhart, pp. 36–39, Office of Air Force History, Washington, D.C. (1979)

Hooton, E. R., *Phoenix Triumphant: The Rise and Rise of the Luftwaffe*, Arms and Armour Press, London (1994)

Horne, Alistair, *To Lose a Battle: France, 1940*, Penguin, New York (1969)

Kesselring, Albert, *The Memoirs of Field Marshal Kesselring*, Presidio Press, Novato (1989)

Kiesling, Eugenia C., *Arming Against Hitler: France and the Limits of Military Planning*, University Press of Kansas, Lawrence (1996)

Kirkland, Faris R., 'French Air Strength in May 1940,' *Air Power History* (1993) Vol 40 nr.1, pp. 22–34

Koch, Horst-Adalbert, *Flak: Die Geschichte der Deutschen Flakartillerie 1935–1945*, Verlag Hans-Hennig, Bad Neuheim (1954)

Lecuir, Jean; Patrick Fridenson, and Général Vuillemin, 'L'organisation de la Coopération aérienne Franco-Britannique (1935–Mai 1940).', *Revue D'Histoire de la Deuxième Guerre Mondiale* Vol. 19 (1969), pp. 43–74

de Lespinois, Jérôme (ed.), *La Doctrine des Forces Aériennes Françaises 1912–1976,* Centre D'études Stratégiques Aérospatiales, Paris (2010)

Lormier, Dominique, *La Bataille de France au Jour le Jour*, Cherche Midi, Belfond (2010)

Maier, Klaus (ed.), Horst Rohde, Bernd Stegemann, Hans Umbreit, *Germany and the Second World War: Vol. 2, Germany's Initial Conquests in Europe* (*Die Errichtung Der Hegemonie Auf Dem Europäischen Kontinent*), Oxford University Press, Oxford (1991)

Martin, Paul, *Invisibles Vainqueurs: Exploits et Sacrifices de L'Armée de L'Air en 1939–1940*, Éditions Y. Michelet. Paris (1990)

Middlebrook, Martin and Chris Everitt, *The Bomber Command War Diaries*, Penguin, London (1985)

Ministère des Armées, *Guerre 1939–1945: Les Grandes Unités Françaises*, Vol. 1, Imprimerie Nationalè, Paris (1967), 1939–1940: Corps, Fortified Regions, and Groups

Ministère des Armées, *Guerre 1939–1945: Les Grandes Unités Françaises*, Vol. 2, Imprimerie Nationalè, Paris (1967), 1939–1940: Divisions

Ministère des Armées, *Guerre 1939–1945: Les Grandes Unités Françaises*, Vol. 3, Imprimerie Nationalè, Paris (1967), 1939–1940: Divisions

Murray, Williamson, *Strategy for Defeat: The Luftwaffe, 1933–1945*, Air University Press, Maxwell Air Force Base, Alabama (1983)

Nielson, Andreas, *The German Air Force General Staff*, USAF Historical Study 173, USAF Historical Division, Maxwell Air Force Base, Alabama (1968)

Olivier, Jean-Marc (ed.), *Histoire de L'Armée de L'Air et des Forces Aériennes Françaises du XVIIIe Siècle à Nos Jours*, Privat, Toulouse (2014)

Overy, R. J., 'Air Power, Armies and the War in the West, 1940', *The Harmon Memorial Lectures in Military History*, The U.S. Air Force Academy (1989), pp. 1–24

Overy, R. J. and Andrew Wheatcroft, *The Road to War: The Origins of World War II*, Macmillan, London (1989)

Richards, Dennis, *Royal Air Force 1939–1945: The Fight at Odds*, Vol. 1, HMSO, London (1974) [1953]

Richey, P. H. M., *Fighter Pilot: A Personal Record of the Campaign in France 1939–1940* (repr. Cassell Military Paperbacks ed.), Batsford, London (2002) [1941]

Ring, Hans and Werner Girbig, *Jagdgeschwader 27*, Motorbuch Verlag, Stuttgart (1991)

Sharp, Lee, et al., *The French Army 1939–1945: Organisation, Order of Battle, Operational History*, 5 vols, Osprey (1998–2002)

Speidel, Gen. Wilhelm, *The German Air Force in France and the Low Countries 1939–1940*, 3 vols, USAF Historical Study 152, USAF: Maxwell AFB (1958)

Taylor, Telford, *The March of Conquest*, Nautical and Aviation Press, Annapolis (1958) (repr. 1991)

Westermann, Edward, *Flak: German Anti-Aircraft Defenses, 1914–1945*, University Press of Kansas, Lawrence (2001)

Wood, Derek and Derek Dempster, *The Narrow Margin*, Pen & Sword, London (1961)

INDEX

Page numbers in **bold** refer to illustrations and their captions.

Abbeville 42, 60, 69, 78, 81, 86
Advanced Air Striking Force (AASF) 29
aircraft
  British
    Armstrong Whitworth Whitley 28
    Avro Lancaster 29
    Bristol Blenheim 29, **30**, 44–45, **53**, 56
    Fairey Battle **29**, 29–30, 38, 44, 52–53, 56–57, **58**, **65**
    Handley Page Halifax 29
    Handley Page Hampden 28
    Hawker Hurricane 29–30, 36–38, **38**, 61, 64, 68, 75–77, **80**
    Supermarine Spitfire 29, 74–77
    Vickers Wellington 28
    Westland Lysander **28**, 29
    see also Royal Air Force
  French
    Amiot 143: 24, **26**, 56
    Bloch MB. 131: **24**
    Bloch MB. 152: **23**, 24
    Bloch MB.200: 24
    Bomber-Combat-Reconnaissance (BCR) 24
    Breguet 690/693: **5**, 45
    Curtiss Hawk 75: **64**, **65**, 80
    Curtiss Hawk P-36: 24
    Dewoitine D.520: 24, **45**, 80, **82–83** (81)
    Douglas D-7: 24, **25**, 80
    Farman NC.222: **43**
    Lioré et Olivier LeO 45/451: 24, 56
    Loire-Nieuport LN.401/411: **66–67** (65), 68
    Martin 167: 24, 80
    Morane-Saulnier M.S.406: 24, **31**, 80
    Potez 63: **6**, 24
    see also l'Armée de l'Air

  German
    Dornier Do 17: 12, **12**, 60
    Fieseler Fi 156 Storch 59
    Heinkel He 51: 13, 18
    Heinkel He 111: 12, **13**
    Heinkel He 177: 17
    Henschel Hs 123: **19**, 58
    Henschel Hs 126: **16**
    Junkers Ju 52: 14, 60, **86**
    Junkers Ju 87 'Stuka' 14, **54–55** (53), 58, **75**
    Junkers Ju 88: **11**, 12
    Messerschmitt Bf 109: **4**, 12, 58, **61**, **79**, **82–83** (81)
    Messerschmitt Bf 110: 12, **14**
    see also Luftwaffe
airfields, Luftwaffe forward 14
Albert Canal bridges, Maastricht 44
Altmayer, General Robert 81
Amiens-Glisy Aerodrome 64
Ardennes, Belgium 42–43, 45
l'Armée de l'Air 13, 23–28, **27**, 31–32, **39–40**
  Zone of Air Operation East (ZOAE) 25, 81, 87
  Zone of Air Operation North (ZOAN) 25–26, **33**, 35–37, 65, **78**, 81, 84
  see also aircraft, French
armistice 88
Arras 60, 68–69

Barratt, Air Chief Marshal Arthur 29–30, **37**, 37–38, 59, 61, 90
Belgian army 41–42
Berlaimont **66–67** (65)
Billotte, Général d'Armée Gaston 68–69
Blount, Air Vice Marshal C. H. B. **8**
bombing offensive, British 62–64
Bordeaux 88
Boulogne 69–71, **77**
Bridges 49
Britain, Battle of 17, 19
British Air Forces France (BAFF) 29–30, **40**

British Expeditionary Force (BEF) 4, 13, 29–30, **40**, 41–42, 68–77
bunkers, concrete 47

Calais 69–71, **75**
Cherbourg 88
Churchill, Winston **32**
Civil War, Spanish 11, 13–14, 18, 20
command and control 12, 90
Condor Legion 13–14, 18, 20
Conseil Supérieur de la Guerre (CSG) 23
Crécy-sur-Serre 59

d'Astier de La Vigerie, General François 30, 35, **35**, 65
de Gaulle, Colonel Charles 59–60, 65, 68
doctrine, Luftwaffe 12–14, 90
Douhet, General Giulio 23
Dowding, Air Marshal Hugh 61
Dunkirk 69–77, **70**, **71**, **76**
  see also Dynamo, Operation
Dutch forces 41–42, 44
Dyle Plan 32, 42, 45
Dynamo, Operation **72–73**, 74, **74**
  see also Dunkirk

Enigma machine 84

Fall Gelb (Case Yellow) phase 8, 42–43
Fall Rot (Case Red) phase 10, 16, 77–80, **78**, 86–88
Felmy, General Hellmuth 43
Fliegerverbindungsoffiziere (Air Liaison Officers) 13, 21, 59
FLIVOs see Fliegerverbindungsoffiziere (Air Liaison Officers)
French Army **39**, 42–43
  First Army 60–61, 68
  Tenth Army 81
  21st Mechanized Corps 56
  4th Armoured Division 59
  5th Cavalry Division 47
  55th Infantry Division 45, 47, 49
  71st Infantry Division 47, 49
French Navy **66–67** (65), 68

Gamelin, General Maurice 23, 30–34, **32**, 41–42, 68, 89
German army
  Army Group A 42–43, 47
  Army Group B 42–43, 44
  Army Group C 42–43
  XVI Motorized Corps 44
  XIX Panzerkorps 45, 47, 52, 69–70
  XLI Armeekorps 45
  1st Panzer Division 45, 49
  2nd Panzer Division 45, 49
  7th Panzer Division 86
  7th Fallschirmjäger Division 44
  10th Panzer Division 45, 49
  Infanterie Regiment Grossdeutschland 45, 49
Göring, Reichsmarschall Hermann 15, 70
Gort, General Lord **32**, 61, 68–69
Guderian, General Heinz 45, 70

Hitler, Adolf 11, 15–16, 42–43, 70
Huntziger, Général d'Armée Charles 56

Ironside, Field Marshal William Edmund **32**
Italy 17–18

Kesselring, General der Flieger Albert **17**, 17–18, 43, 90
Kleist, General der Kavallerie Ewald von 43, 45

La Chambre, Guy 25
Lainé, Lieutenant Francis 65
Lancastria, RMS 88
Le Havre 88
Lille 71
Loerzer, Generalleutnant Bruno 48
Londonderry, Air Commodore **36**
Luftfahrtministerium (Air Ministry) 11, 16, 20
Lufthansa 16
Luftkreisschule (Air District School) 11
Luftkriegsführung (Conduct of the Aerial War) 12
Luftstreitkräfte (Air Force) 11
Luftwaffe 11–14, 43
  Luftflotten (Air Fleets) 12
  II Fliegerkorps 48, 87
  VIII Fliegerkorps 12, 19, 48, 52, 58–60, 69–72, 75, 79

Flak Regiment 102: 49, 52, 56–57
  see also aircraft, German; *Fall Gelb* and *Rot* phases

Maginot Line 23, 29, 41–42
Manstein, General Erich von 42
Merville airfield 64
Meuse River 45
  see also Sedan
Milch, Generaloberst Erhard **15**, 15–17, 79, 89
Mölders, Hauptmann Werner **82–83** (81), 91
Montcornet 59, 65

Netherlands 44–45, 61–62
Newall, Air Chief Marshal Cyril **36**, 36–37, 89
night flying 18–19
North Africa, aircraft evacuated to 88
Norway 16

Orders of Battle
  British 40
  French 39–40
  German 21–22

paratroop landings 44
Paris 84–86, 87–88
Paula, Operation 84–86
Pétain, Marshal Philippe 23
plans captured, German 42
Playfair, Air Marshal Patrick 29–30, **36**, 37–38, 90
Poland 14, 16, 17, 20, 41

radar 75, 85
radio communications **85**, 85–86, **87**
rail network, attack on 88
Reinhardt, Generalleutnant Georg-Hans 45
Richtofen, Generalmajor Wolfram von 14, **15**, 18, 19–21, 48, 70, 90
Rotterdam, Netherlands 61–62
Royal Air Force 28–30, 40
  Bomber Command bases **63**
  and Dunkirk evacuation 74–77
  2 Group 52
  11 Group 74–81
  No. 3 Squadron 53
  No. 12 Squadron 56
  No. 105 Squadron 56
  No. 142 Squadron 56

No. 150 Squadron 56
No. 218 Squadron 56
No. 226 Squadron 56
  see also aircraft, British
Rundstedt, Generaloberst Gerd von 42

Saint-Nazaire 88
Schlachtflieger (battle planes) 13
Schwartzkopff, Oberst Günter 53
Sedan 4, 42, 43, 47–57, **50–51**
Seeckt, Generaloberst Hans von 19
ships, evacuation **71**, **74**
Sperrle, General der Flieger Hugo **18**, 18–19, 43, 48, 90
strategies, opposing 41–43

tactics, Luftwaffe 90–91
tanks
  Char B heavy tank 52, 56
  Matilda heavy tank 68
  Panzer II 47
technicians, French NCO 24–25
training 90
Trenchard, Air Chief Marshal Hugh 28

Udet, Generaloberst Ernst 17

Vitry Airfield 64
Vuillemin, General Joseph 24, **25**, 34–35, 89

weapons, anti-aircraft
  British
    3.7in. heavy anti-aircraft gun 30
    3in. anti-aircraft gun 30, **56**
    Bofors 40mm anti-aircraft gun 30, **91**
  French
    25mm light anti-aircraft gun 85, **89**
    75mm heavy anti-aircraft gun 85, **89**
  German
    20mm flak gun **57**, **60**, 91
    88mm flak gun 20, **20**, 91
Wever, Generalleutnant Walther 17
Weygand, General Maxime 34, 68, 69